The Lammas Drave
and the Winter Herrin'

The *Launch Out,* ML 455, and *Ivy Leaf,* ML 166, in Pittenweem harbour.

The Lammas Drave and the Winter Herrin'

A History of the Herring Fishing from East Fife

PETER SMITH

JOHN DONALD PUBLISHERS LTD
EDINBURGH

ISBN 0 85976 125 8

Typeset by Key Phototypes, Edinburgh.
Printed in Great Britain by Bell & Bain Ltd., Glasgow.

Acknowledgements

In preparing this book, for which I did research over a period of more than thirty years, I have been indebted to a large number of people who have given me the benefit of their knowledge and experience.

The number of fishermen who answered my questions with unfailing patience and regularity are too numerous to thank individually, but I must mention some of them. Alex Smith of St Monans, now aged 95, and Alex Motion of Cellardyke, approaching 98, were my authorities on the sailing boats, as were my father and his brother David. Jockie Gay, a native of Pittenweem, now 81, was the authority on the sma' lines and jigs, while my experts on the steam drifters were my late friend George Muir, whose diary of 1938 appears in Appendix IV, his brother James Muir, James Brunton and my school classmate Tom Anderson. On the small boat side, although not claiming to be an expert, I was my own authority, having gone to the creels and anchor nets in my family's three sailing yawls and two motor yawls in which I was brought up.

I also wish to thank the many Fishery Officers who helped me; John Lawson, D. Swanney, P. Logue and James Tarvit. The latter gave me a list of figures which tallied with mine except for 1935 and 1936 when the fishings lasted longer than normal and the returns were in Edinburgh before the end of the fishing. James Tarvit was also of great assistance with the Glossary. I must also express my gratitude to the late C. Russell, the last proprietor of the *East Fife Observer*, for allowing me to take home bound copies of his newspapers to peruse at my leisure.

I also wish to thank all those who helped with the photographs, particularly Bill Flett who allowed me access to some of the photographs taken by the late George Cowie of St Andrews; the Scottish Fisheries Museum who gave me permission to use their dark room; and John Doig who gave up his spare time to print the majority of the photographs. I am very grateful to the following who gave permission to use their photographs in the book: Scottish Fisheries Museum, Anstruther for pages ii, 3, 6, 9, 11, 15, 21, 27, 37, 38, 47, 51, 57, 61, 65, 71, 77, 79, 82, 85, 93, 105, 113, 117, 126, 129, 133; National Museum of Antiquities of Scotland (Easton Collection) for pages 2, 5, 7, 13, 14, 17, 23, 29, 33, 35; W. Flett (Cowie Collection) for pages 41, 69, 75, 89, 96, 101 and for the illustration used on the cover; J. Watson for page 135; Mrs G. Smith, Pittenweem, for page 44; J. Brunton for page 110; James Miller for page 25; Mrs David Smith for page 120; James Wood, St Monans, for page 50; and David Wood for page 54.

I would also like to thank Robert Gardner for allowing me to take extracts from his great grandfather's diary and Mrs George Muir for taking extracts from her husband's diary for 1938.

Peter Smith

Selected Scottish Port Distinguishing Marks

A   Aberdeen
AA   Alloa
AH   Arbroath
BA   Ballantrae
BF   Banff
BCK Buckie
CN   Campbeltown
DE   Dundee
FR   Fraserburgh
GN   Granton
INS   Inverness
KY   Kirkcaldy
LH   Leith
ML   Methil
ME   Montrose
PD   Peterhead
RO   Rothesay
TT   Tarbert
WK   Wick

Contents

Introduction

This book traces the rise and fall of two local herring fishings. The Lammas Drave, which took place off the coast of East Fife in August and September, reached its peak in 1860, whereas the winter herring fishing in the same area, which took place in the three months January to March, reached its peak in 1936, and had practically disappeared in another ten years. The summer fishing staggered on till 1914, but most of the local boats preferred to fish in the North, once they had fully decked boats.

The passing of the winter herring fishing was blamed on the ring net and seine net, but there may have been other causes. In a paper, 'Fisheries, Scotland, Sci. Invest., 1937, No. III', page 38, there is a sketch of the East Coast of Scotland, with an arrow pointing to the Firth of Forth, and originating from an area east of Wick. As this is near the Fladen ground where herring were caught by trawl, the herring shoals may well have been destroyed there. Another paper, issued by the Fishery Board for Scotland in 1936, states that the good fishings of 1934 and 1935 were caused by two different races of herring. This they established by the number of vertebrae in the back bone, and also the keeling scales of the herring.

The Fishery Board maintained an office in Anstruther until 1973, when the Fishery Officer moved to Pittenweem. He was in charge of the East Fife Area, from Buckhaven to the Tay, and the statistics I quote were obtained from the local Fishery Office. Buckhaven at one time had the second largest fleet in the District, after Cellardyke, but the Wellesley Colliery at Methil was probably the chief cause of its decline. It provided alternative work, with the attraction of a steady wage. The refuse from the pit was dumped into the sea, and this 'redd', as it was called, gradually engulfed the harbour, until it no longer exists now. Their last two motor yawls at the winter fishing in the 1930s were the *Maggie Deas* and *Iris*. The excellence of the sailing qualities of their boats can be gauged from Lubbock's book, *The Log of the Cutty Sark,* where he says that Linton, the designer of the *Cutty Sark,* was influenced by the underwater lines of the Buckhaven boats.

St Monans was the next of the full-time fishing ports east of Buckhaven. During this century they had a few steam drifters, but they stuck to their 60-70 ft. motor boats, converted from sailing boats, much longer than the other local ports. They also had a larger fleet of 35-55 ft. motor bauldies than the other ports. These latter boats were the best adapted for the winter herring fishing. The steam drifters and large motor boats fished at the winter herring with drift nets of 18 score meshes deep. The smaller motor yawls and sailing yawls fished at the anchor nets with nets of 9 score meshes deep, but the bauldies fished at drift or anchor nets, according to wherever the herring could be found. This they did with nets of 12 score deep.

St Monans, having more bauldies than the other local ports combined, had therefore the best fished boats on average at the winter herring, between the two wars. They still have a boatbuilding yard, and the firms of Miller, Reekie and Robertson served East Fife well. The last-named firm, which preceded Reekie, built the *Elspeth Smith,* the last of the big motor boats in St Monans.

Pittenweem is now the centre of the East Fife Area, having the only market, and its Fishery Officer is in charge from Alloa to the Tay. Pittenweem moved ahead of its rivals for the first time in 1948, when its total earnings exceeded £21,500, with Crail having just over £21,000, Anstruther £12,000 and St Monans £9,000. Pittenweem was the last stronghold of the sma' line fishing, which was still being pursued there in the 1950s, getting mussel bait from the Eden estuary. In bad weather they used to put booms across the inner harbour entrance for protection, and for this reason their larger boats and bauldies fished from Anstruther during the winter herring fishing.

Anstruther has the largest harbour in the East Neuk, but very few fishermen lived there before the last War; even the few I knew then had been born in Cellardyke. Most of the steam drifters in the East Neuk had Cellardyke skippers and crews, and if the St Monans bauldies were the top local boats at the winter herring fishing, the Dykers were the top men at the great line fishing, and also at the Great Yarmouth herring fishing, as they could go to sea in weather that kept the largest motor boats in port.

Crail is the last of the East Neuk ports, the home of the lobster and partan fishermen. Their contribution to the winter herring fishing this century was mainly at the anchor nets, and it seems likely that their motor yawl, *Comely,* was the last to try the anchor nets in 1947.

Only small catches of herring were landed in Methil, St Andrews and Tayport. The Methil landings were by the steam drifters when up there for coal; St Andrews entirely from the anchor net; and Tayport by the ring net.

Appendix I is an extract from one of my father's poems published in 1951.

Appendix II contains extracts from a diary kept by Peter Murray (Venus Peter) of Cellardyke from 1866 to 1891. The diary is now in the possession of Robert Gardner, his great grandson, of Cellardyke.

Appendix III contains extracts from articles in the *East Fife Observer,* in 1927, by 'Auld Wull'. He was William Smith, who died in 1931, aged 82, having retired in 1922 as Port Missionary in St Andrews.

Appendix IV contains extracts from a diary kept by George Muir of Cellardyke, in 1938, when he was in the steam drifter *Spes Aurea,* of which his father, John Muir, was skipper. This diary is now in the possession of the Scottish Fisheries Museum, Anstruther.

Appendix V contains statistics from the Fishery Office.

The Early Years

Apart from the three major Statistical Accounts, general statistics were only kept by law in Scotland from 1855. It was necessary for earlier sources to be investigated. In East Fife we had Jack writing about St Monans, and Gourlay writing books about Anstruther and Cellardyke. The latter was given to quoting Lamont, who appears to have belonged to Largo. On reading the only copies of Lamont's diary I could get, I was still puzzled about the early history of the fishing in the East Fife area. I also consulted a book called *The Sovereignty of the Sea* by Fulton and gleaned from his writings the following details. In East Fife, which consists of the ports from Buckhaven to St Andrews, an important fishery took place in the early part of the twelfth century, shared by the men of England, Flanders and France who paid tithe to the monks on the Isle of May, whose monastery was founded in the time of David I.

In 1641, Charles I changed the tithe (paid in herrings) into a money tax. These taxes seem likely to have been paid for landings of herring in the months of July, August and September, partly because of the weather and partly because of the quality of the herring.

Dunbar was a more important landing place than Anstruther for the summer fishing, known as the Lammas Drave; and in the seventeenth century it was estimated that as many as 20,000 people would congregate in that area either on sea or land, in connection with the fishing.

As the fishing was from open boats (they were undecked until the 1860s), not many herring would be landed during the winter, and it was said that ten centuries ago the winter herrings were used chiefly for bait.

To summarise what we do know about the fishing before the First (Old) Statistical Account in 1799 written mainly by the ministers, we have, according to Gourlay's books:

1550-1655 good fishing

1657-1693 no fishing

1693-1780 good fishing.

From the First Statistical Account we gather as follows:

Anstruther Easter: '1799 population about 1,000. In 1710 it was made a port having its own custom house, being formerly a creek under Kirkcaldy. In 1768

1

Fifie sailing boats leaving St Monans harbour.

the shipping tonnage was 80 tons, and 1,400 tons in 1799. Shipbuilding was being carried on to a considerable extent.' Fishing is not mentioned.

Anstruther Wester: 'Cod, ling, turbot, halibut, skate, haddocks, herrings, flounders and lobsters are caught here and sent to Cupar, Edinburgh, Stirling and Glasgow. Lobsters are the only fish sent to London, from which it is supposed that about £1,000 is annually brought into this and neighbouring towns. Once every 2 years, the sea weeds growing on the rocks are cut and burnt into kelp. 10 tons is thought a good produce for the 2 years—population 370. Decay of the town was due to union with England.'

'Before the Union twenty-four ships belonged to Easter and Wester Anstruther, and thirty boats at the Fishing. At present the total is twenty ships and one fishing boat. There is not one single fisherman in the parish, yet in the herring season i.e. summer season there are four boats manned by tradesmen.'

Parish of Kilrenny: 'The fisheries are now miserably decayed. There used to be no less than fifty large fishing boats belonging to Cellardyke (6 men in each boat) fishing for herring in the summer season. Population—1,086.'

Buckhaven boats at Shields for the summer herring fishing season, sometime last century.

Parish of Pittenweem: 'Population 1,157. Fishing declined. Fish sent to Edinburgh market, Lobsters to London.'

'The population increased considerably within the last 25 years, owing to the colliery and salt works of Sir John Anstruther, which made up for the decline in the fisheries, there being only 12 fishermen, but 36 miners. Prices of provisions doubled within the last 30 years.'

'Kelp is made here, averaging 8 tons yearly. Parliament has passed a bill for turnpike roads in Fife, and a great road from East to West will pass by the town.'

Parish of St Monance: Before 1646, the name of the parish was Abercrombie. It was sometimes called St Menin, St Monan, St Monans and at present St Monance. 'Population—832. Great scarcity of haddocks as well as herring. There are fourteen large boats and twenty small boats, which latter are used all the year round for white fishing—4 men for the oars and 1 steersman. The larger boats are used only for herring, with crews of 7 or 8 men. There are also some yawls worked by a man and a boy. They fish with the hand line for codlins. The young men go whaling but return for the summer fishing.'

Crail: Carle, Caryle, Carraille is supposed to signify, in the Gaelic, its situation upon a small winding and bending of the shore.

'About the beginning of this century Crail was the rendezvous for the herring fishing in the Firth of Forth. The Drave was seldom known to fail but for half a century the fisheries here have been declining; due partly to the encroachments of the Dutch who occasionally sweep our coast with a fleet of nets extending several miles in length at no greater distance than 2 or 3 leagues from the shore, and partly to the industries of man having thinned this species of fish. This also appears to have contributed to the want of haddocks. About 20 or 25 thousand lobsters are sent every year to the London market. 10 years ago there was double the number. The price was £12.10s. the thousand. The population is 1,710. There belongs to this port six sloops from 25 to 60 tons; one brig of 150 tons; one sloop upon the stocks. These vessels employ 25 men. Six boats are engaged at the white fishing; six smaller ones at the lobsters employing in all 45-50 men. In 1791, thirteen large boats with crew of 7 were fitted out for the herring fishing.'

May Island: 'there were formerly 10 or 15 fishermen's families. Now only 3 men and 2 women looking after the light.'

Fife Ness: 'There is only one boat with 2 fishermen.'

Wemyss including East and West Wemyss and Buckhaven. 'Many have left the fishing because of scarcity of the haddocks. Formerly there were five boats with a 5 man crew in East Wemyss and one boat in West Wemyss. Now only one boat in East Wemyss. About 40 years ago, 25,000 haddocks were landed in Buckhaven in one day. Today most of the fish go to Edinburgh. Buckhaven has twelve boats, with crew of 6. They used to go in August to fish for herring at Dunbar; but have now abandoned it because of small returns. There are 140 families, of whom 60 are fishers.'

Valuable as these statistics are, they are dependent on the interests of the chroniclers, who certainly keep us very ignorant of East Anstruther and Cellardyke. However, there are some figures in Sibbald's *History of Fife* of 1710:

St Monans had ten fishing boats with a 4 man crew at the white fishing, and twelve boats with a 7 man crew at the herring.

St Monans harbour. In the foreground are newly tarred ropes. They were tarred once a year.

Pittenweem six boats with a 6 man crew at the white fishing. Fifteen boats with a 7 man crew at the summer drave.

Anstruther Easter put out twenty-four boats to the summer drave.

Cellardyke ten boats with a 6 man crew at the white fishing all the year round. Twenty boats with a 7 man crew to the summer drave.

The year 1800 saw a disaster at Cellardyke harbour, when a boat was upset and six of the seven crew were drowned in sight of their families. Gourlay, in his book *Monks and Fishermen,* gives a graphic description of the disaster. He also tells us that the boat involved was one of the seven Cellardyke boats engaged that spring in the great line fishing: 'Then as now herring bait was indispensable for the big hooks; but the drift being undreamed of it was fished according to ancient custom by nets anchored perhaps within hail of the shore.'

From 1783 to 1816 fishings were poor. Some of the best fishers among the young men had been pressed, of course, for the Navy by the press gang, and only on their return after the end of the Napoleonic Wars did the fishing begin to recover.

James, William and Peter Smith. Peter, the author's grandfather, was the second son and in the East Fife tradition was named after his maternal grandfather, Peter Murray, who died at Wick in 1829 while at the fishing. They are wearing the fisherman's rig of inner and outer waistcoats of pilot cloth. The inner waistcoat was the length of a short overcoat and was worn inside the trousers, which had a buttoned flap at the front.

From 1816 to 1822 the herring draves during the summers were very successful locally, and in the latter year the herring were so numerous they were sold to the farmers to manure the fields.

From 1822 to 1836 the herring fishings were a failure.

The East Fife District was certainly not one of the leaders in the industry of smoking fish, and it seems unlikely that they smoked haddocks much before 1819, which date seems to be the time when they first made bloaters after the Yarmouth style.

The steam drifter *Camellia* and Fifie sailing boats in St Monans harbour. KY 221 is the *Sincerity* and KY 658 the *Fyalls*. She later had an engine installed and was renamed *Brighter Dawn*.

The departure of the herring shoals from the summer drave in the period 1822-36 meant that the fishermen had to go further afield, both to the lines and the summer fishings. In 1826, on her maiden voyage to the great lines, one of the Cellardyke boats, *Victory,* was lost within sight of the May Island, with seven of her crew, there being one survivor. She was 34 ft. long and said to be the leviathan of the fleet, and had made the number of the bigger boats up to twenty-four. Not until the 1880s did the local boats approach 50 ft. in length, and many of those advertised for sale in the *East Fife Record,* which began in 1855, were only 38ft. in length.

Gourlay tells a story of this time in different ways in his separate books on Cellardyke and Anstruther, but the essence of it is this: A Cellardyke boat, the *Box Harry,* had gone out to shoot her anchor nets for herring bait in February 1826, and saw a good appearance of herring in the deeper water. Not being in their larger boat which would carry a chauffer fire which they would use when out all night during the summer drave, the crew were reluctant to try the drift nets as they would have to be attached to them all night. It should be remembered that these were undecked boats and remained so until the 1870s, and the cold would be severe. However, they shot their drift nets and the result was a great success. The following year a large shoal set in off Pittenweem which was successfully exploited by the Pittenweem fishermen.

The Pittenweem and St Monans men seem to have been the mainstay of the winter herring fishing as it now became, until a great storm in 1833 made the fleet run for shelter to Elie and the mouth of the Cocklemill Burn, but alas three Pittenweem boats and one St Monans boat were lost in this terrible calamity, with the loss of 19 fishermen. This had so great an impact on that area that the large sum at that time of £2,000 was collected for the widows and orphans.

The winter herring were lacking in fat and would not cure properly, and so the winter herring fishing remained relatively unremunerative until the advent of the railways brought new buyers from England. That was some time off, and news about the fishing is not easily come by.

The last series of successful summer fisheries, known locally as the Lammas Drave, was now about to begin and lasted roughly from 1836 to 1862, after which it never really recovered, partly from scarcity of herring and partly because with larger decked boats it was more profitable to follow the shoals from Shetland to Lowestoft.

From a letter dated 1836 from George Smith to J. Dunsmure we get the following:

10th August: 'twelve boats have been regularly fishing about the May Island catching 3, 4 and 5 thousands, for which they were getting 4s. per hundred from the cadgers. The herring were full, fat and fine, and more was expected.'

26th August: 'four boats had from 10-15 crans each, caught close in at a depth of 8 fathoms.'

8th September: 'some boats arrived with herring from Holy Island'—but by 22nd November—'some of the fishermen's families were starving.'

And now for the first time from the Fishery Office records we get a few details of a winter herring fishing; brief as they are, I will give them:

1837

25th January: three boats had 5 crans each, but the general catch was from 1½-5 crans; prices 20s. to the hawkers.

An East Fife sailing bauldie.

21st January: twenty-five boats landed 1-5 crans, although the wind shifted into the East. More cod than for 20 years.

28th February: forty boats landed herring, of which four got 5 crans each, while the others only got hundreds. Prices were 26s. for some and the rest for manure.

6th April: for the year ended March 1837, the total cured was 3,927 barrels.

7th August: twenty-three boats averaged 10 crans for the week.

12th August: thirty-five boats totalled 1,090 crans. No salt as the curers were unprepared, expecting to go to other parts, so the prices were only 11s.-16s. per cran. Seldom as good quality seen on the east coast of Scotland.

24th August: one boat 50 crans in the Auld Haikes (between Fife Ness and Kingsbarns) and all the boats anchored their nets there in the daylight, getting catches of 30, 40 and 50 crans, leaving some nets anchored as the boats could not hold any more. Prices fell to 8s. per cran.

25th August: greatest ever, catches from 20-70 crans. Prices 8s. per cran. Fishing in the daylight. Fortunately a sloop arrived with salt, and prices rose to 13s per cran.

The total cure was 22,200 barrels.

1838

27th January: twelve boats averaged 2½ crans, prices 25s. per cran.

1st February: St Monans is mentioned for the first time by the Fishery Office. St Monans had twenty-two boats averaging 4 crans at 25s. per cran, while Cellardyke had four boats averaging 4 crans.

2nd February: seventy boats averaged 8½ crans at 27s. per cran. Highest catch 21 crans.

3rd February: eighty boats averaged 20 crans, prices 16s. per cran. Highest catch 38½ crans.

5th February: seventy boats averaged 5 crans at 15s per cran. Highest catch 34 crans.

6th February: one hundred and thirty boats averaged 13 crans at 10s.-11s. per cran. Highest catch 40 crans.

8th February: one hundred boats averaged 2½ crans. Highest catch 10 crans.

9th February: one hundred boats averaged 11 crans. Highest catch 15 crans. (No prices given for last 2 days.) Herrings shifted from the May and have gone up the Firth. Good fishings off Buckhaven and Largo.

The harbour, Anstruther, from the east end of Shore Street in 1873.

14th March: Monday's average 2½ crans, Tuesday averaged 1½ crans. Plenty of herrings, but intense frost.

15th March: S.E. gale and Cellardyke pier damaged. The total cure was 4,408 barrels.

26th July: fifty-four boats averaged 2 crans, quality and appearance good.

28th July: sixty boats averaged 2 or 3 crans, good appearance, water too still.

1st August: Tuesday seventy boats averaged 2½ crans at 25s. per cran. Wednesday averaged 2½ crans, highest 11.

6th August: Wednesday seventy boats averaged 2½. Thursday averaged 4. Friday averaged 3. Saturday averaged 1½ crans.

8th August: seventy-six boats averaged 5 crans.

9th August: highest 35 crans, great fishing, even better at Pittenweem and St Monans; good quality.

15th August: Thursday averaged 10, Friday averaged 12, Saturday averaged 10. Monday averaged 5, Tuesday averaged 3, Wednesday averaged 11.

20th August: last days of last week, uncommonly heavy fishing. Some over 60, and average 35 crans per boat. Good quality from the Auld Haikes, prices 7s. per cran to the curers.

25th August: averaged 25, highest 57; best in Scotland at present 7s. per cran.

29th August: quality excellent. Curers at a standstill. Curing in tan pits and boats. Some boats with 60 or 70 cran shots were sent to Leith and Burntisland, at prices of 8s. 6d. and 9s. per cran. Some boats have caught individual totals of 500 crans.

3rd September: unprecedented. One boat totalled over 600 crans for the season.

21st September: fishing over. Eighty local boats averaged totals of 350 crans.

1839

29th January: Highest catch 18 crans. Fishing up the Firth before this.

30th January: Highest 16 crans.

2nd February: Averaged 10, highest 30.

15th February: Stormy Monday, eight boats averaged 4 crans, Tuesday, nineteen boats averaged 6 crans.

19th February: Monday, fifty boats averaged 5 crans near May, prices 16s.-17s. per cran.

20th February: Sixty-three boats averaged 14 crans near May, breezy with much loss of nets.

27th February: Monday averaged 4 crans, Tuesday averaged 5, Wednesday, eighty boats averaged 6 crans at 18s. per cran.

2nd March: Thursday and Friday, averaged 15 crans at 14s. per cran from one hundred and thirty boats, highest 30 crans.

That concludes the information in the form of copies from letters.

A *History of Fife,* up to 1840, was published by Leighton, and the information in it is very similar to that in the Second (New) Statistical Account published in 1845.

Cellardyke or Nether Kilrenny had 300 fishermen out of a population of 1,800. One hundred large boats (13-18 tons). The boats cost £100 each and nets cost £5 each. Each boat fished with 14-20 nets, the crew being three or four regular fishermen with one or two half dealsmen.

In 1839, the total catch locally was 25,000 barrels of herring. Seven hundred barrels of pickled cod to London and seven hundred to Liverpool. Three thousand barrels of smoked haddocks to Glasgow, Liverpool and Manchester. The herring seasons were January and February, August and September.

In the other months, 28-30 boats went as far as 40-50 miles to the white fishing, manned by eight men each, the owner getting a double share. The haddock lines are baited with mussels from the Eden, a cartload costing 20s.-22s. Usually thirty boats went as far away as Wick. Anstruther Easter and

St Monans fishermen preparing their gear for a new fishing.

Wester provide very little information about the fishing in the Second
Statistical Account. For example, Wester says 'no fishermen in this Parish'.
Easter records 600 barrels of cod cured annually; 6 fish curers; 11 vessels, 2
packets sailing between there and Leith. Total population of the two
Anstruthers about 1,500. Pittenweem in this same survey had a population of
1,349 and a considerable number of fishing boats, but as Anstruther Easter had
a better harbour, the fishing was chiefly connected with that part. A few
sloops or schooners are recorded.

The ministers who wrote the reports for Pittenweem and the two
Anstruthers gave few details about the fishing compared to the fuller reports
given for St Monans and Cellardyke, but Leighton's book gives Anstruther
Easter one hundred boats with five men each, and states that Pittenweem is one
of the creeks of Anstruther Easter and that their boats are included therein.

St Monans is very fully covered compared with its neighbours in the
Statistical Account. The population is given as 1,110. 'Fishing is the chief
occupation in this parish and affords work to 300. The lines are baited by the
women. There is a partial winter herring fishing, but in the summer they put
out twenty-six boats of 15 tons each and valued at £85 each. Each boat has 20

The gear being put on board ready for a new fishing. KY 340 is the *Helen Wilson.*

nets costing £4 each. The net is 50 yds. long 15 score meshes deep, each mesh being 1¼ inches.'

'Many of the boats go as far as Caithness, when they are engaged for 6 weeks, the bargain being understood to be completed on catching 250 barrels. Cured cod is sent to London and Liverpool. Haddock, turbot and cod to

Buckhaven harbour in 1894. Among the sailing bauldies are *Gratti the Leader,* KY 505, owned by J. Deas and the *Harmonious,* KY 62, owned by T. Warrender.

Edinburgh. The creek also has fourteen yawls of 7½ tons each, with a schooner of 78 tons and a sloop of 40 tons.'

Crail had a population in 1841 of 1,765. 'Last year, viz. 1844, they had only twelve boats, and only sent 4,000 lobsters to London and 3,000–4,000 dozen crabs to Dundee and Edinburgh. They also exported 50 tons of wilks.'

Wemyss Parish claimed a population of 5,000. It certainly included East and West Wemyss as well as Buckhaven of which latter creek it was said there were 170 fishermen and one hundred and forty-four fishing boats of various dimensions. 'In July they go North to Helmsdale, Fraserburgh and Wick for about 2 months. There are sixty first class boats costing £75 each, with nets valued at £110 each. There are forty-four second class boats costing £40, with nets valued at £120 each. There are forty third class boats costing £14, each with nets valued at £20 each.'

The reason for the value of the nets belonging to a second-class boat being greater than the value of the nets of a first-class boat is that the second-class boat worked with three sets of nets and the first-class boat with only two sets of nets.

The other source of information about this period around 1850 was the *Pittenweem Register,* which was published from 1844 to 1855.

1845

'March 1st—The herring fishing just closed was generally large. The price in Pittenweem was as high as 25s. per cran.'

Only occasionally does the fishing get mentioned, as it was printed on one column of a single sheet. The Lammas Drave did set in strong however, and on August 30th we hear that 'on Saturday last at Pittenweem most boats had excellent hauls, one had 85 barrels, but it was difficult to get enough workers for curing them'.

The town crier with his bell was sent round the town offering extra inducement to the women as gutters, and into the night every station was lighted with numerous candles. The shoal was in the area known as the Treath or Traith only about one mile from the harbour. The fishing boats were lighted up and there was no time for rest. Shots as high as 70 barrels were recorded, and Anstruther harbour was equally busy.

September 6th— 'Up to this day, Friday, more heavy hauls were made, and the fishing was far superior to anything in the last two years. The sea, about a mile from Pittenweem, is covered with boats from all quarters. Anstruther and St Monans have had the same success, one St Monans boat had 65 crans. Prices have been 12s. to 14s. per barrel. The steam packet *Stirling Castle* brought over 50 or 60 women from Fisherrow to help with the curing.'

September 13th—The Drave was now ended; on the whole successfully.

1846

No reports of the winter herring were given, and the Summer Drave was below average until August 22nd. 'The takes of herring were very lively last Saturday. An extensive drove had stationed themselves opposite Pittenweem harbour, and the boats belonging to St Monans, Pittenweem and Anstruther plied them well. Many of the boats had three good shots that day; and they continued the work until a late hour on Saturday evening. A number of French luggers are lying opposite and on either side of our harbour, employed in the herring trade.' There were also eight or nine French luggers lying in and about Earlsferry containing twelve men each.

September 29th—'The fishing this week has been the most successful for the last 20 years and excellent quality. On Monday night last an extensive drove was discovered on the south side of the river to the eastward of the Bass, and as many boats as had gone there came in with full cargoes. The boat of Andrew

Washing the ballast stones after a fishing, to freshen up the bilge water. The round blue stones used for ballast were brought from the south west side of the May Island where they had been smoothed by friction from the sea. All the local boats got their ballast there. Nowadays, concrete is used for ballast.

Anderson (B) brought in the extraordinary haul of 108 crans. On Thursday the whole shore of Anstruther was literally covered with heaps of herring. Everyone is employed that can work. The shores of Cellardyke, Anstruther, Pittenweem and St Monans are fairly covered with barrels of herrings, and almost every hour the fishing boats are bringing in additional supplies.

Prices are down to 5s. per barrel with the market glutted.'

September 19th—End of the Drave. Crail boats averaged 100 barrels each. For other local places the average was nearer 300 barrels each.

October 3rd—'A sign of the success of the late Drave was shown in the number of marriages that have recently taken place; viz. Cellardyke 16, Pittenweem 20, St Monans 16, Buckhaven 19.'

1847

February 6th—'A goodly quantity of herrings taken this week. Prices varied from 20s. per cran on Monday to 10s. per cran on Saturday.

'In St Monans, the boat of William Marr caught 13 barrels of herring while another boat was charged 6s. per 100 by a Buckhaven boat for bait.'

February 13th—'Frost was so severe that smoke from Auld Reekie (Edinburgh) appeared only 4 miles away. Fishermen in open boats were so cold they could hardly speak when they came home.

The fishing was not so good as the previous week but the boat of Andrew Heugh had 12 barrels of herring at 12s. per barrel.'

February 20th—'Herring fishing was unproductive this week and the fishermen are thinking of giving up the fishing.'

'Messrs Todd, fishcurers, Anstruther, purchased herrings on Tuesday last, caught that morning at the May, converted them into red herrings and sold them in London on the following Friday.' (The railway did not reach Edinburgh until the next year.)

August 14th—'Well fished on Friday 5-25 crans each.'

'Thursday, a Crail boat had 47 crans from the Auld Haikes. There are now fifty-six luggers off the coast.'

August 21st—'Some excellent hauls were got at the Auld Haikes last week.'

September 4th—'Tuesday, fishing general, 5-10 barrels each. Wednesday, fishing disrupted by gale.'

September 11th—'On Friday night, last week, while the fishermen of Crail were off their guard and lying comfortably in bed, a fleet of Cellardyke boats came and caught from 4 to 40 barrels each just opposite Crail harbour.

The Dykers are like marine bloodhounds; they follow the herrings by their scent.'

September 18th—'Although the average catch in the area was thought to be good, only 4 marriages were reported this year, compared with the larger number last year.'

December 18th—'A violent gale from the N.E. caused great damage to the boats in the local harbours. During the hurricane the tide was 8ft. above normal.

'At Pittenweem, the house on the shore called the Island was certainly an island that night, and the houses on the west shore were flooded.'

1848

January 26th—'The herring fishing improved considerably this week, and on Tuesday one boat had 22 barrels in Anstruther and every boat got less or more.'

February 26th—'The winter herring fishing is now over in this district and it is considerably under average.'

May 13th—'A new Low Water pier opened at Pittenweem.'

July 1st—'A new iron steamer *Xantho* being built on the Clyde for Anstruther costing £3,600.'

July 29th (1st week of Drave for 1848)—'Best this morning is 6 barrels, some got very few, but all got puckles. Those who went to the South got least.'

'Prices 16s.-20s. per barrel.'

August 5th—'On Tuesday, some boats upwards of 50 crans, none less than 1½. Prices as low as 7s. a barrel. Wednesday, some boats very heavy laden and the herring are of superior quality, with fishing going on in the daytime as well as night. Prices 10s. a barrel. Thursday, as prosperous as on the other days. One St Monans boat already exceeded 200 barrels. Price 8s.'

August 19th—'The fishing during the week was languid.'

August 26th—'The fishing went on but slowly. A violent storm on Friday night scattered the boats, but on Monday morning the St Monans men were out early, but met one boat coming in with 80 barrels.

During the present week the most sanguine expectations of the fishermen have been fully realised and the shores of the various towns along the coast are literally covered with fish, of a most excellent quality.'

'The school of herrings are in the Fluke Hole opposite Pittenweem. Prices 10s.-11s.'

September 2nd—'Tuesday evening last looked stormy, and a number of boats did not leave the harbour. Some of those who ventured out were well rewarded for their toil, but suffered severely in loss of nets.'

September 16th—'Drave now over for the season. Crail had bad success and the marriage market dull, but Cellardyke, Pittenweem and St Monans, brisk.'

1849

February 10th—'The commencement of the winter herring fishing was very much retarded by the stormy state of the weather, which even caused the new Anstruther steamer *Xantho* to run for shelter in Elie, but during the last and present week, several good shots have been got, some boats having as much as 10 barrels, prices 12s.-20s. a barrel.'

February 24th—'Last Saturday the fishing was more successful, a Cellardyke boat had 40 barrels and a Pittenweem boat had 15, while 100 barrels were landed at St Monans that day. Tuesday and Wednesday were crowned with success and the present season is expected to be above average. Price was now down to 9s.'

March 3rd—'The Pittenweem boat *Mary,* skipper Andrew Heigh, was lost with all 7 of the crew. A hurricane dispersed the fleet, some running as far as Kirkcaldy for shelter. The boat was last seen near the Bass Rock about 3 a.m. This, the first winter herring after the railway came to Edinburgh, made no mention of improved markets as Gourlay implied in his books.

March 10th—'The aftermath of the loss of the Pittenweem boat disclosed that no St Monans or Pittenweem fishermen were members of the Shipwrecked Fishermen's and Mariners' Society (annual subscription 2s. 6d.) but 60 Cellardyke fishermen were members.'

July 28th—'The favourite station opposite Pittenweem has been crowded with boats every night this week, the best catch being by a St Monans boat with 14 barrels, prices 15s.-21s. a barrel. The Dealers are coming here to purchase for the Edinburgh market, as the herring are cheaper than at Dunbar and the fares are not more than half.'

August 11th—'On Thursday boats were well fished, the average catch along the coast being 14 barrels, from the fishing ground east of Crail.'

August 18th—'By Wednesday the boats were on their favourite area opposite Pittenweem (California) and on Thursday our shores were literally covered with herrings, some boats exceeding 60 barrels. Excellent quality and prices down to 8s. 6d. a barrel.'

August 25th—'Fishing so abundant, that its like has not been seen in East Fife, but prices fell to 4s.-5s. per cran'. (The word cran definitely used here instead of barrel.)

September 1st—'The fishing is so plentiful that a number of curers are fully satisfied. Unfortunately the prices have fallen so low that it does not pay the fishers at 3s. per barrel.'

September 8th—'The Drave is nearly over although still plenty of herrings in the Firth, but prices are too low to encourage the fishermen.'

September 15th—'The fishing which had been given up for want of barrels and salt has commenced again and large quantities of herring have been brought into all the fishing towns on our coast, prices being 5s. 6d. per cran.' (The word cran again used.) 'No person now living has any recollection of so plentiful a fishing.'

1850

January 19th—'No boats at sea for the last fortnight, because of an east wind with snow 1ft. deep. Worst weather for 3 years.'

Sailing boats in Anstruther harbour about the end of last century. These were the last of the big sailing boats.

February 23rd—'One boat had 30 barrels, and every one got less or more' (phraseology for general).

March 2nd—'Extraordinary success of herring fishing. The herring are plentiful and of good quality. More like summer herrings; four or five steam tugs are engaged in carrying herring to Leith and the local steamer *Xantho* has been making double trips. In ordinary winter fishings 10 or 12 barrels is considered a good shot, but this time the boats are bringing in from 20 to 50 barrels. Fishing of this present season has never been surpassed and rarely equalled. Prices are from 8s.-13s. a barrel.'

March 16th—'The herring fishing is now over, but the boats are now catching as much turbot, cod, skate and haddocks as they can carry so depressing the prices that turbot was 2d. a lb.'

March 30th—'Pittenweemers are now calling the Fluke Hole or Treath, California because of the large amount of herring taken there in recent years.'

April 27th—'There was a riot in St Monans because of the success of 2 trawl net fishermen in the Treath.'

July 27th—'Herring partial but of excellent quality; all bought by cadgers. An order has been received at the Custom House, Anstruther, to seize any boat without name and number.'

August 3rd—'Three or four French luggers keep up prices to 11s.-12s. a barrel. 40 barrel shot in Anstruther was the highest this week.'

'Two St Monans boats went out at 9 p.m.; thinking it was midnight, as there was no town clock.'

August 17th—'The fishing improved, but not general, with great loss of nets.'

August 24th—'Last Saturday there was an average of 50 barrels from the Auld Haikes bringing prices down from 7s. to 3s. 6d. a barrel, but not much since.'

September 7th—'The half dealsmen are leaving in despair.'

September 14th—'Heavy fishing at last with best shot of 98 barrels in Anstruther. 40, 50, 60 cran shots quite common. Prices 3s.-9s. a barrel for cured herring, but that finished the season.'

October 19th—'An interesting story from Earlsferry where there were no regular fishermen. 'A crew of half dealsmen killed 200 barrels at the drave in only 3 shots, and all on Saturdays, thus proving that Saturday is still lucky for Earlsferry men. (Macduff was said to have been ferried to the Lothians on a Saturday.')

1851

February 15th—'An immense quantity of herring was taken during the last 8 days, at prices of 10s. a barrel. (Alas that was the only mention of the winter herring fishing that season.)

July 19th—'The second week of the Drave began when 200 boats set out from the three ports of Cellardyke, Pittenweem and St Monans, and steered eastward but the best catch was only 5 barrels at 21s. a barrel.'

August 2nd—'The 3rd week of the Drave saw two hundred boats fishing in California, the area about 1 mile off Pittenweem: It is described as 2 or 2½ miles in length from opposite the Billowness westward to St Monans. Some heavy shots were landed, with 40 barrels the highest shot at 10s.-12s. a barrel.'

'Wednesday saw heavy landings, the fleet having been joined by the Crail fleet.' (The names of the boats were never mentioned, but the skippers were. For example, that day the boat of D. Marr Jnr of St Monans had 50 barrels, A. Gay, 39, J. Hutt, 26, A. Scott, 22, R. Mackay, 30, G. Hughes, 31, A. Spence 28, Andrew Hughes, 33, and Joseph Butters, 11. Prices 9s.-11s. a barrel. Many of these names can still be found in Pittenweem and St Monans.)

August 9th—'The fishing continued very unequal, but all the boats got less or more. Two Cellardyke boats, skippered by a Murray and a Watson were

Setting down the nets in the hold in preparation for another night's fishing. The man on the left is mending his net right up to the last minute.

the first to a total of 200 barrels; only one Pittenweem and one St Monans boat had managed 100 barrels by this time.'

August 16th—'The fishing was poor during the past week.'

August 23rd—'No sign of a general fishing. Prices 9s.-12s. 6d. a barrel.

September 13th—'Half dealsmen left in despair. The fishing now considered a failure and the trawlermen of St Monans were getting the blame for destroying the spawning beds. Large quantities of salt and 30-40 thousand empty barrels are scattered over the 3 towns.'

1852

February 7th—'The winter herring fishing has now been in operation for the last fortnight; and a few boats have had good shots.

The main rendezvous for the boats is Anstruther, as the local steamer *Xantho* and a steam tug are carrying cargoes of herring to Leith.

English merchants here based their representatives at Anstruther, and the *Xantho* is connecting with the rail service, as quickly as if the railway were at

Anstruther. The greater competition from buyers, means better prices being offered than at neighbouring harbours. The prices are high from 12s.-20s. a cran, even as much as 38s.'

February 28th—'During the last fortnight a considerable quantity of herrings have been taken, but never enough to overstock the market.

'On Tuesday last skipper Tarvit had 30 barrels and skipper Scott 24; both belonging Cellardyke.'

March 20th—'The fishing up to Thursday was very unequal; but then the herrings congregated about ½ mile off Pittenweem and about 1 mile East and West of the town.

'The boats were so near the land the fishers could be seen hauling their nets. A great quantity of herring was caught at prices of 25s.-35s. a barrel. The tide being suitable the *Xantho* had them in Edinburgh by midday. Good catches of white fish were landed as well.'

March 27th—'The herring fishing was now finished and the boat of Skipper Corstorphine caught and carried to Montrose the enormous quantity of 11 cartloads of cod, ling and skate and 1 load of turbot.

April 3rd—No mention was made of the success or otherwise of the recent fishing, but a meeting was held in Pittenweem, where it was resolved to send a deputation to the Fishery Board to try to stop the use of the destructive trawl net in California.

August 7th—'The start to the Lammas Drave saw some good shots but not a general fishing. High prices to cadgers and steam boats—14s.-20s. a barrel.'

August 14th—'The best fishing was East of the May Island, with an average of 5 barrels in Anstruther and 2 in Pittenweem, prices 14s. a barrel.'

August 21st—'Most fish caught this week near the Bass Rock and nothing from East of May Island. Prices 15s.-16s. a barrel.'

'Saturday the 21st was the best day of the season with the best shot 50 barrels—Price 12s.'

August 23rd—'Several boats went out last night and this morning' (the only evidence for suggesting that the boats went out on Sunday).'Those that went out first got good shots at Dunbar, but the later boats got few. Best shot in Pittenweem was 24 barrels at 12s. a barrel.'

August 27th—'The best day's fishing of the season; all from the south side and of excellent quality. The average in St Monans was 40 barrels, in Pittenweem 50, and in Anstruther 35, bringing prices down to 10s. a barrel.'

August 28th—'From the fishing ground between North Berwick and Dunbar, another good fishing, but not as good as yesterday. The average in the 3 ports was 17 barrels, price 10s. a barrel.'

The launch of a bauldie built by Miller at St Monans before the First World War.

By September 1st the shoals had gone and so had the half dealsmen, and overall, the fishing was regarded as a failure, not much better than the previous year. Once again the trawl in the Fluke Hole or California was blamed for destroying the spawning ground.

1853

No information about this year, nor the winter herring fishing of 1854.

1854

(Some more statistics are now appearing, but this is counterbalanced by less information about the fishing grounds.) August starts with the news that the local fleet comprises three hundred and thirty-five boats, Anstruther and Cellardyke one hundred and five, Crail six, St Andrews three, Pittenweem fifty-four, St Monans sixty, Largo and Methil six, Buckhaven one hundred and one. (The reason the last was so seldom mentioned was that the boats fished mainly on the Dunbar side during the summer and ventured to Shields outside the herring season.)

August 5th—'Very good quality, prices 26s.-35s. a barrel, highest 8 barrels.

Buckhaven boats at Dunbar, but thirty-four French boats anchored off Anstruther.'

August 12th— 'The boats were regularly at sea all week; one third of the fleet fishing by day and meeting with a fair success, but criticised by the rest for injuring the fishing ground.'

August 26th—'The fishing was very heavy during the last 3 days, highest shot being 93 crans, prices 13s. a barrel.'

Septemer 2nd—'Good takes from the south side, best catch 50 barrels. Spent amongst them. Prices 10s. 6d.-15s. a barrel.'

September 9th—'Heavy fishing, night and day. Prices down to 3s.-6s. a barrel.'

September 16th—'The season is now over, and one of the best ever. The 105 boats of Anstruther and Cellardyke Averaged 328 barrels.

54 boats of Pittenweem averaged 251 barrels.

60 boats of St Monans averaged 205 barrels.'

(This totals over 60,000 barrels, so Buckhaven must have had about 8,000 barrels landed there, as the total for the District was given as 68,000. This somewhat confirms the fact that the Buckhaven boats fished mainly at Dunbar.)

1855

The first year of compulsory record keeping in Scotland saw a winter herring fishing that was said to be below average. January saw from sixty-five to eighty boats fishing from Anstruther and about fifty fishing from Buckhaven. By February as many as one hundred and fifty boats were fishing from Anstruther; but catches were not very good, and the fishing was said to be better up the Firth all season; 40 barrels was the highest catch mentioned, with prices from 24s.-40s. per barrel. The fishing came to an early end, mainly because of the weather. On March 3rd it was said that it was the most severe and protracted frost for the last 20 years, having lasted for more than 5 weeks. The total for the District was 4,000 crans. This year was also the last of the *Pittenweem Register,* as the printer J. Scott died. However, during the summer he had doubled the size of his paper and so increased the amount of news of the fishing, so we may as well make the most of it, as this was to be the second best Lammas Drave on record.

May 19th—'The 16 curing stations at Pittenweem were sold, with the dearest being £6.'

The steam drifter *Nancy Hunnam* with a Cellardyke crew, among them J. McRuvie, W. Kermack, J. Deas, A. Watson, J. Watson, P. Smith, (the fisherman poet of Cellardyke) and C. Gen, (Chairlie the Frenchman).

June 2nd—'Anstruther East Pier (present Middle Pier)'to be widened by 40 ft. inside the harbour to accommodate fish curers during the Lammas Drave.'

June 23rd—'A Cellardyke chimney fire, set fire to the thatch of two adjacent houses.'

July 7th—'Anstruther fish curing stations were rouped for a total of £139. 10s.'

In 1854, the sum received from rouping the curing station had been £83; in 1853, £64: in 1852, £28. 10s., so we can see that expectations were rising.

July 23rd—'The whole fleet from the three local ports went to sea at the beginning of the week, comprising one hundred and fifteen boats from Anstruther and Cellardyke, fifty from Pittenweem and fifty-six from St Monans, plus the Buckhaven boats, which numbered one hundred, the latter fishing mainly at Dunbar. The maximum number of boats landed locally was three hundred and thirty, so some stranger boats had also been present. Although the *East Fife Record* was now in existence, I will take most of the information about this fishing from the *Pittenweem Register*.

July 25th—'Most of the boats went south and east, and almost every one got a few. Prices 32s. a barrel. The fishers report that there is a great appearance of fish. The sea is filled with 'baffers' (porpoises, I think) 'which was a good sign, and whales were seen in the vicinity of the May.'

August 10th—'The fishing of this day was general, and of good quality.'

'The fishing ground extended from California to the May. The shots ranged from 4 to 34 crans. Prices 14s.-16s. a cran.'

August 11th—'A capital fishing. It was general and of the very best quality. The average at Pittenweem was upwards of 20 barrels. Anstruther and St Monans had the like good fortune. The highest in Pittenweem was 36 crans at 12s. a cran.'

August 14th—'An immense quantity of fish brought in. The fishing was general. Shots of 30-50 barrels were numerous. The fishing ground was California.'

August 15th—'Another good fishing, but as the boats were all crowded together in California, there was a great loss of nets. One boat lost 14. Shots ranged from 10 to 70 crans. Price 12s. a cran.

August 18th—'The fishing of this day was very unequal. Very little off Pittenweem, but shots of 20 to 50 crans came from the south side. Price 12s.'

Monday, 20th August —Notice reached Cellardyke on Sunday that herring had set in at the Auld Haikes (the North side of Fifeness). This induced the boats' crews of that town to leave harbour at an early hour on Monday morning, and they came home throughout the day heavily laden with fish. The crews of Pittenweem and St Monans were later on the scene, but they also returned with full cargoes. The quality was good and prices 8s.-10s. Unfortunately disaster struck one of the boats when a gale sprang up in the afternoon, and the boat of Adam Reid, Cellardyke, was lost off Crail with the loss of four men.

21st August—'There never was a greater quantity of herrings brought into the harbours in this neighbourhood at any former period. The shots ran from 40 to 80 crans and were general. The fishing ground was the Auld Haikes, which has not been destroyed by the trawl net. This large catch brought the price down to 6s. a cran.'

Wednesday 22nd August—'The fish had shifted and the boats came home clean.'

Monday 27th August—'Nearly the whole fleet of boats went to sea early this morning and the majority were rewarded for their vigilance. The shots ran from 10-20 crans. Prices 10s.-12s. a cran'.

Thursday 30th August—'The best day's fishing for the week. The whole fleet went to the eastward of May Island, and an immense quantity of fish was taken. The highest was 80 crans and prices were 6s.-10s.'

Tying on the nets in St Monans. This operation went on in dry weather in the back streets of the town. Spikes were driven into the ground to support the legs which held the ropes at waist level to facilitate the tying on. When the streets were tarred, in the 1920s, this operation was forbidden and the nets had to be tied on in the garrets, doubling the ropes back and forward.

Saturday 1st September—'Small takes but general. The fishing ground extended from the Heuch (Kincraig) eastward to the May Island. The heaviest shots came from the east, the best being 24 crans, excellent quality. Price 10s.'

4th September—'The fishing ground extended from the Heuch to Fifeness. Those at the extreme ends got shots from 10 to 30 crans. Those opposite Pittenweem came in clean. Prices 11s.-15s.'

6th September—'The heaviest shots came from the eastward, the best being 98 crans. Prices down to 9s.'

12th September—'No fish worth speaking of, and with the half dealsmen leaving the Drave appears to be over, and at that there never was a better Drave.'

September 25th—A great appearance of herring having been seen for some days past, a number of Cellardyke boats went to sea and shot their nets off Crail and came in the next day with very fair takes, the highest being 35 crans at prices 12s.-14s. a cran, but this time it was the end of the Drave, and the number of barrels of cured herring was given as: Anstruther 36,000; Pittenweem 14,000; St Monans 12,000.

The total catch for the District was given as 75,000, so Buckhaven was producing as much as St Monans, although fishing mainly at Dunbar. So ended the second greatest Lammas Drave, and with rumours of 40 impending marriages we close the descriptions of the fishing scene from the *Pittenweem Register,* with the report of a new paddle steamer being launched at Leith for the Anstruther and Leith Shipping Company. She was 128 ft. long with engines of 75 H.P. and named the *Forth.*

1856

The fishings were poor in 1856 and very little is known. Nevertheless, some statistics are available, although not for the winter herring fishing.

Anstruther and Cellardyke could put one hundred and thirty-seven boats to sea employing 728 men of whom 333 were non-resident. The value of the boats was put at £7,000, the nets at another £7,000, and over £2,000 worth of lines. Pittenweem owned fifty boats employing 200 men, 75 of whom were non-resident. The boats were valued at £2,000, the nets £1,800, and the lines £250. St Monans had ninety-nine boats employing 396 men, 132 non-resident. The boats were valued at £4,000, the nets nearly £5,000 and the lines over £3,000.

In this year Anstruther and Cellardyke put out to the Lammas Drave one hundred and fifteen boats, which averaged 52 crans; Pittenweem fifty-one boats averaging 82 crans, St Monans fifty-four boats averaging 80 crans. The total catch, therefore, for this year was just over 16,000 crans, hardly half the average of the last ten years. (This is certainly news, as we only have figures for the last two years, and I am afraid that is all I know about 1856.)

1857

This year saw an earlier start than usual to the winter herring fishing, and on 16th January one hundred boats landed 450 crans in Anstruther; prices were 32s.-40s. a cran. The best fished boats were from Buckhaven as half their nets were cotton, and were longer and deeper than the nets made from hemp.

January 31st—One hundred and eighty boats were now fishing from Anstruther and forty to fifty between Pittenweem and St Monans; the stranger boats came from Broughty Ferry, Buckhaven, North Berwick, Prestonpans, Newhaven, Fisherrow and Dunbar.

February 25th saw the best day's fishing when ninety boats landed 1,100 crans in Anstruther. Prices were 25s.-28s. a cran. The next day saw a total of 800 crans followed by 400 and 250 cran totals, this being the main week of the season; the fishing closed about the middle of March. Anstruther's total was about 7,000 crans, while 9,135 crans was the District total, valued at £16,443.

May 30th saw thirty local boats landing 250 score of white fish, mainly haddocks, from 70 miles away. The boats were only partially decked, and carried a crew of eight men, who each had 15 taes of line, each taes having 120 hooks (the sma' lines').

The Lammas Drave opened with fine weather, and on August 8th there were two hundred boats fishing in the Treath (alias California or the Fluke Hole to the Pittenweemers); fifty were from Pittenweem and sixty-nine from St Monans. It was proving another poor fishing, and on August 22nd, in very warm weather, a lot of the herring were damaged before they got to the local ports from the fishing area on the south side of the Firth.

The week finishing August 22nd was the only good week of the season, when about one hundred and twenty boats brought in successive totals of 336, 570, 1,250, 540 and 2,400 crans, the prices staying above £1.

The season closed by mid-September, with 23,000 crans for the District; one hundred and twenty Anstruther and Cellardyke boats averaging 75 crans; forty-nine Pittenweem boats 93 crans; and sixty-two St Monans boats 113 crans.

The average price was £1 a cran, which caused much comment, and *The East Fife Record* gave what they usually did not do, the average prices for the previous two years. Average price for 1856 was 12s. 6d. a cran, and for 1855 it was 11s. a cran.

1858

February 20th—'The fishing was quite good, in reasonably good weather. It was equally successful at the west stations, Pittenweem, St Monans and Buckhaven. The Buckhaven fleet is expected next week, as the fishing generally takes off up the Firth at this time.'

On this day seventy-eight boats landed 700 crans at 26s.-29s. a cran, the best catch being 35 crans. This was the best day's fishing of the season, and the total for the district was 11,220 crans valued at £19,076, of which Anstruther and Cellardyke had 6,000, Pittenweem, St Monans and Buckhaven each having in excess of 1,000. This was regarded as a good general fishing for this time (there were still no fully decked boats) and the prices were also regarded as very good. The herring when bought went all to home markets and were either slightly salted or made into bloaters.

August 21st—The Lammas Drave started well, with a good general fishing at Pittenweem and St Monans as well as Anstruther, whose figures for August 18th were seventy boats landing 2,450 crans at 16s. a cran, the average at Pittenweem and St Monans being between 30 and 35 crans.

August 28th—The fishing continued to be good, with St Monans boats fishing better than the rest. Several boats were having two takes in one day, and during this week the catches in Anstruther were as follows:

Tuesday—230 boats landed 1,380 crans; prices 19s.-20s. a cran

Wednesday—235 boats landed 2,115 crans; prices 16s.-19s. a cran

Thursday—230 boats landed 230 crans; prices 11s. a cran

The fishing continued good right up to the middle of September and resulted in the third best Drave on record, with a total of 70,544 crans for the District from three hundred boats, valued at £50,000. The one hundred boats of Anstruther and Cellardyke averaged 242 crans. The fifty-three boats of Pittenweem averaged 230 crans. The sixty-two boats of St Monans averaged 292 crans.

1859

The winter herring fishing of 1859 was plagued with bad weather. This could be seen in the prices, which did not fall below £2 a cran until the first week of February. The day when the most boats were mentioned was February 16th, when one hundred and thirty boats landed only 65 crans at 35s.-38s. a cran. The best day's fishing was February 24th, when fifty-five boats landed 330 crans at 30s.-34s. a cran.

March 19th saw a storm which sprang up so quickly from the south east, combined with a tide that did not come in as quickly as expected, that there was a pile-up of boats at Anstruther in what we now know as the ghats (the outer harbour at Anstruther was not yet built). Many of the boats were on the rocks, but two yawls were launched to take ropes to the stricken boats, and as the tide flowed the crowds on the piers hauled the boats into the harbour by main force. Much damage was done but no lives were lost. As the whole town was turned out for the rescue, this created an outcry for the port to have a lifeboat of its own.

The total catch for the District was 7,860 crans, Anstruther having 4,047 crans. By August 20th the Lammas Drave had got off to a good start, with the

A boat being launched by block and tackle. She is not a newly-built boat but one which has been laid up on shore.

St Monans boats leading the way. Already 4,000 crans had been landed in the District compared with only 1,200 the previous year, and prospects looked good. However, things did not turn out like that, and the week ending August 20th was the only good week. The one hundred boats fishing from Anstruther had three successive days of 1,000, 2,000, 2,250 crans, but as the fleet increased the catches decreased, and the best day's catch, after a few mediocre weeks, was 800 crans on September 9th at 21s. a cran, the prices of the good week having been down to 9s. a cran. This was certainly a poor year compared to the previous one:

    Anstruther and Cellardyke had 150 boats averaging 70 crans

    Pittenweem had 62 boats averaging 78 crans

    St Monans had 68 boats averaging 114 crans

The total for the District was 28, 379 crans.

'Auld Wull', who wrote in the *East Fife Observer* of 1927 about Cellardyke seventy years previously, said that in the early 1860s the fishing changed, the inshore fishing fell away, and the boats had to go further afield to seek for herring; the boats therefore got larger and the smaller boats were of little use.

1860

The *East Fife Record* is the source from which most of our facts will be taken. The fishing was prosecuted up the Firth for the last four or five weeks by a fleet of fifty-four boats. By January 28th, it was cold and drizzly, with some rain and some snow. On the Thursday, ninety boats averaged 2½ crans, highest 8 crans, total 225 crans. Prices ranged from 38s. to 40s. per cran.

By February 4th, some strangers were arriving. On Wednesday, one hundred and twenty boats (many strangers) averaged 3 crans, highest 33¼ crans, total 360. Prices were 35s.-37s. per cran. The total for the year in Anstruther at this time was 1,524 crans, while for the District the total for the year was 3,850 crans, which meant that Pittenweem, St Monans and Buckhaven together were exceeding Anstruther at this time.

The report for February 11th mentioned clear moonlight (which was not liked), strong tides and severe frost. Taking Friday as the day when most boats landed, we have one hundred and four boats, average 2½ crans, highest 12 crans; total 265 crans, prices 40s.-42s. per cran.

February 25th—one hundred stranger boats fishing from the East Fife ports, making a total of two hundred and twenty boats fishing off the coast from Buckhaven to Crail. This week saw favourable weather and fishing mainly near the May Island. Thursday seems to have been the best-fished day; one hundred and forty-five boats landed in Anstruther, average 4½ crans, highest 20 crans, total 697 crans, prices 22s.-26s. per cran.

March 3rd—bad weather and not many boats out until Wednesday night, so the Thursday landing was one hundred and two boats averaging 2 crans, highest 16 crans, total 204 crans. Anstruther's total now appears to be 7,274, compared with the District's 11,674, so it would appear that the fishing at Buckhaven must have eased off and most of the catch was now being landed from Anstruther to St Monans.

March 10th—strong tides and clear moonlight bothered the fishing, the best landings being on Thursday, when fifteen boats averaged 3½ crans, highest 12 crans, total 50 crans, price 33s. per cran.

The winter herring fishing was nearly closing, although on March 17th it was mentioned that some St Monans boats had over 20 crans on the Tuesday. By the end of the month the whole area had finished, with Anstruther's total being 8,276 crans compared with 4,047 in 1859, while the District totalled 13,950 crans compared with 7,946 in 1859.

It should be mentioned here that most of the boats would be undecked, although there would be a few half-decked ones among them. Since this was to

A boat being hauled up by traction engine. She would have been used for the summer fishing only and would be laid up on shore until the next summer when most of her crew would be halfdealsmen from the Highlands or the Fife coal pits. Only the best boats went south to Scarborough, Gt Yarmouth or Lowestoft.

be the peak of the Lammas fishing on record, it might be interesting to mention some of the other features of this remarkable year.

It was said to have been the longest and most severe winter for 25 years, half of the autumn of 1859 was winter. The coldest day was February 14th, when 13°F was recorded at Airdrie House. February saw only four nights without frost and March only five. June turned out to be wet, with the crops looking good. Potatoes always get a mention, as there had been disastrous losses in the 1840s from blight.

As the Lammas fishing approached, Anstruther and Cellardyke mustered one hundred and seventy-three boats, about 40 ft. long compared with thirty only 25 ft. long in 1830, when the whole cure for the District was 1,589 barrels.

July 28th—Lammas fishing commenced. Breezy, and only half the boats went out. Herrings reported everywhere from the Bell Rock to Elie Ness. Excellent quality. Thursday of that week was the best, when one hundred boats averaged 4½ crans, total 458, prices 18s.-24s. per cran. Anstruther and Pittenweem had a bounty of £5. This was a sum of money paid over by a fish curer on striking a bargain with a fisherman to supply him with an agreed amount of herring at a fixed price. The practice had died out by the beginning of the twentieth century.

By August 11th, after moderate fishing, the first Irish boat was in the Firth. Friday was the best day, 160 boats, average 9 crans, best 42, total 1,440, prices 20s.-24s. per cran, 3,608 crans for the week. Dunbar at this time was full of boats, highest 60 crans, prices 20s.-22s.

Now we come to the week ending August 25th, which we must consider in more detail, as it was never to be surpassed in local records; since records were kept accurately only from 1855, we can only guess at the great fishing of the late 1830s and 1840s.

On 21st August every boat seemed quite loaded as it entered the harbour at an early hour, and as soon as discharged immediately put to sea again for a second shot, returning in the afternoon with as many as it could take on board. Quality was excellent. In Anstruther alone two hundred boats averaged 45 crans. Pittenweem and St Monans were similar. News came ashore on Monday that there was an immense shoal in the Treath (off Pittenweem), and there were four hundred boats there before sunset. No less than 16,500 crans were caught within range of three or four miles off Anstruther, worth £16,000 to the fishermen and £22,000 after curing. Here are the details. On Tuesday 21st August, two hundred boats averaged 45 crans, highest 90, total 9,000, prices 12s.-16s. per cran (the week's total was 15,000 crans). The week ending September 1st produced a claim that Monday's average was the highest then recorded in Scotland. Monday 27th August, one hundred and forty boats averaged 60 crans, highest 93, total 8,400, prices 8s.-12s. per cran. There was then a gradual tapering off, and by September 8th half-dealsmen had gone home and only a few spent herrings were landed. Great fishings had also been landed at Dunbar, and it was noted that two Buckhaven boats foundered with herrings in the swell off North Berwick.

Anstruther's Lammas fishing was 38,000 crans compared with 10,000 crans the previous year, and the District landed 83,000 crans compared with 27,865 crans the previous year, a total never to be surpassed even by the winter herring fishings of 1935-36.

1861

January 19th—Boats had been successful up the Firth but there was a south-east gale, at the mouth of the Firth. At Pittenweem, fourteen boats averaged 8-14 crans.

The Cellardyke drifter *Olive Leaf*, later sold to St Monans where she was renamed *Casimir*. Among the crew on deck are J. Cunningham, J. Smith, D. Tawse, D. Dick, D. Smith, J. Murray and W. Smith.

January 26th—Buckhaven boats had been well fished, but herring were reported to be moving down the coast. On the Saturday, sixty boats averaged 3½ crans in Anstruther, prices 33s.-36s. The weather was still not good in the mouth of the Firth, but there was good fishing up at Buckhaven. The weather continued stormy, but it was noted that the Buckhaven boats had already grossed £9,000. Anstruther's best day in the first week of February was the Tuesday when sixty-one boats averaged 14 crans, highest 46, prices 28s.-30s. February continued mainly stormy, but the fishing appeared to be good when the boats got to sea.

Friday, February 23rd—Sixty-five boats averaged 14 crans, prices 28s.-33s., and 1st March was claimed to be the best ever winter herring day in Anstruther. One hundred and fifty-five boats averaged 10½ crans, total 1,628, prices 12s.-15s.

Two to three hundred boats were now fishing off the local towns. There was much destruction of the light cotton nets, which were introduced by the Buckhaven men. They fished better than the old hemp nets, and so began the use of white nets for the winter herring, as they caught better. They were dipped in boiling alum water to kill the rotten matter which had accumulated in the nets during the week's work.

Gales and storms continued to be troublesome; the season closed at the end of March with a total for Anstruther of 10,718 crans compared with 8,576 the

Pittenweem harbour entrance showing the booms on the pier and the crane for hoisting them into place. They were used to protect boats in the inner harbour during stormy weather.

previous year, while the District had 20,130 crans compared with 14,465 the previous year.

By July 6th, the local boats had gone to fish from Gourdon and Stonehaven while waiting for the possibility of a local Lammas fishing, which had always been erratic. But by the end of the month, one hundred boats were fishing from Cellardyke and Anstruther, although the herring seemed to be distant and lack of wind bothered the boats. Anstruther, Cellardyke, Pittenweem and St Monans together mustered some two hundred and fifty boats, Largo fifteen and Buckhaven one hundred and twenty. Herring were mainly got near Bell Rock and were easier to land at Gourdon and Stonehaven. The best of the season that far was Friday August 2nd, when forty boats averaged 9 crans, price 23s.-27s. Some Penzance boats appeared, having heard of the good fishing the previous year.

Friday, August 9th—Ninety-three boats landed 605 crans in Anstruther, and 2,200 crans among the three ports of Anstruther, Pittenweem and St Monans.

Wednesday, August 14th—Herring were reported in Haikes (i.e. between Carr Rocks and Kingsbarns), and one hundred and thirty-three boats landed 532 crans in Anstruther, but a south-east gale came and bothered them in Haikes. This, however, did not affect Dunbar, which averaged 20-40 crans per boat, one Penzance boat landing 100 crans. Because of this stormy weather, Dunbar boats had beaten the East Fife boats all season.

The week ending August 31st was to prove successful in East Fife, as the herring set in two miles off Pittenweem, and with the winds west to north-west, two to three hundred boats fished night and day, landing a total of 13,000 crans in the three ports that week. One boat had 70 crans and gave six nets away which produced a further 30 crans. The best day was Wednesday, August 28th, one hundred and sixty boats averaged 15 crans, prices 21s.-23s. But by the end of the first week in September the shoals had gone

Pittenweem and St Monans were the best fished ports of the season. The District had 35,100 crans compared with 83,000 the previous year.

At Dunbar, fishing continued all Sunday within gunshot of land, the catch being sold to Irish sloops at sea, as the boats were not allowed to land it.

By the end of September, the Buckhaven and St Monans men were using the beam trawl in the Treath. In November, there was an article about the effects of the beam trawl on the spawn of the herring, and the St Monans men were said to have sold herring spawn to the farmers for manure at 1s. per cartload. (The spawn was not seen in the sea after five weeks.)

1862

Winter herring started promisingly, with Buckhaven men doing well about Inchkeith. There were reports of landings in Burntisland. After a moderate January as many as seventy boats were fishing from Anstruther, and there was a notice saying that the Port of Anstruther was now placed under Kirkcaldy District by the Fishery Board.

By the second week of February, the herring were said to be on the Hirst, that rocky area between Crail and the May. Stranger boats fished well there, some with three hauls in a night, but the average was poor, two hundred boats landing a total of 350 crans, prices 33s.-40s.

Storms of wind and snow saw March come in with one hundred and forty-three boats averaging 6¼ crans, the best of the season, prices 20s.-22s. March remained stormy and the fishing tapered away to a District total of 6,000 crans, nearly 5,000 down on the previous year.

The time before the Lammas fishing started was occupied by line fishing, both by great lines and small lines, and there is a report of one curer smoking 1,700 dozen haddocks for the Glasgow market, while twenty-five yawls were at the creels. (Interesting, as the creels were seldom mentioned at this time.) By the end of June the bigger boats departed for Gourdon and Stonehaven, and by the middle of July some boats had started the local Lammas fishing.

As in the previous year, the herring were first got well east of May Island, and not much was landed locally in July. By the end of the first week in August most boats had returned from Gourdon, and by August 15th, Friday, Crail boats got herring in the Haikes. One hundred and twenty boats averaged 11 crans here on August 12th, 19s.-20s. per cran. St Monans and Pittenweem were also well fished. On the Saturday, August 16th, one hundred and forty boats averaged 50 crans, total 7,000, price 16s. per cran, mainly from Haikes. Nets were lost as the boats came in, some loaded to the gunwales from the Haikes. Pittenweem and St Monans boats were not there, but went down later only to find that they were too late. So that notable date of August 16th, 1862 was the last major catch recorded in one day in Anstruther and ranks alongside the 9,000 crans of August 21st, 1860. Unfortunately these totals were never to be repeated, far less exceeded, in all our history. The District produced 25,000 crans compared with 35,000 the previous year.

1863

There was very little doing in the first fortnight of January, but there were good landings up the Firth where a large shoal set in off Burntisland. Two Findochty boats arrived. It was an open winter up to the end of January, with an average amount of storms. By the middle of February, seventy to eighty stranger boats were reported at the fishing, and by Tuesday, February 17th, one hundred and seventy boats landed an average of 5½ crans in Anstruther, total 950, prices 14s.-17s. This proved to be the best day of what turned out to be a very mediocre fishing which finished really at the end of February, totalling 5,800 crans compared with 6,000 the previous year in Anstruther.

The District's total was 12,750 crans, presumably representing Fife ports from Buckhaven eastwards. At the end of March appeared the report of Professor Allman, who had led an inquiry into the Firth of Forth fishing the previous year, using Royal Navy divers and dredges: '1st appearance of herring in Firth of Forth was the last week in October 1861, but fishing did not begin until 1st week of January, 1862 and up to the end of January, all fish full. (2) No

Fifie bauldies and motor boats in St Monans harbour. Among them may be seen the *Providence, Celtic, Vigilant, Express,* and *Harvest Moon,* ML 15.

spawn found in Firth by dredging. (3) On 1st February, some spent. (4) No Spawn found in Traith from 10th–28th February either by diving or dredging. (5) 1st March, spent herrings in abundance near Isle of May. (6) 1st March spawn obtained 14½–21 fathoms on east and west sides of May Island. (7) Spawn on stones, shingle, gravel, old shells, coarse shell, sand, and even on shells of small living crabs and other crustacea, and it adhered tenaciously. (8) No spawn in any other part of Firth. (9) Spawn continued east and west of May Island up to 13th March and embryo free. (10) On 25th March scarcely a trace of spawn. (11) Nearly all adult fish had left the Firth. (12) No spent until 65 days after they first appeared in Firth and incubation over in 25–30 days.' (Spawn lives after being detached.)

A note about haddocks: On May 16th some boats had 250–350 dozen at 6d. per dozen.

May 30th—Jig herring at the May, as high as a cran, selling at 3s. 8d. per 100.

Again the first summer fishing of Lammas Drave saw local boats at Montrose and Stonehaven, but according to Gourlay's book *Monks and Fishermen,* the Cellardyke boat *Hope* (skipper unknown) made her first summer voyage to Great Yarmouth, following the Fisherrow men.

Again first local catches for the summer came from the Bell Rock area. A few crans went for bloaters, the rest fresh. A listing of the local boats at the Lammas Drave is as follows: Anstruther and Cellardyke 173, Pittenweem 55, St Monans 105, Largo 15, Buckhaven 130, Crail 4, St Andrews 8, total 490.

August 1st—A field of bere, fully ripe, was cut on the Isle of May. There was great want of rain, and it was a poor fishing season locally, although Cellardyke boats were well fished at Montrose. Not until the middle of August did the local boats come home from Stonehaven and Montrose, when they fished in the Treath from where, on August 14th, one hundred and seventy boats landed 520 crans in Anstruther, 16s.-18s.

The next week a shoal was reported in the Haikes, and on August 20th, one hundred and sixty boats landed 280 crans in Anstruther, 15s.-18s. Pittenweem and St Monans were also well fished. Anstruther's total was 6,000 crans compared with 14,000 the previous year. The District only managed 12,300 crans. One important event occurred on 2nd September: the railway arrived at Anstruther Wester.

1864-65

Nothing very significant happened locally in these two years. Fishings were poor. In 1864 maximum fleets of one hundred and twenty to one hundred and fifty boats produced a total of only 3,000 crans compared with 5,000 of the previous year, while the summer fishing produced its last five-figure total ever of 14,000 crans. The weather did not help, as they were stormy winters.

1865 was also poor, and the local boats gave up the herring fishing before the middle of March to pursue the small line fishing for haddocks. One hundred and twenty boats were fishing and produced a total of 5,000 crans for the winter herring fishing. Again they went early to the haddock fishing, prices 7s. per 100. By July they were making ready for the Lammas fishing when the numbers of boats were given as Anstruther and Cellardyke 173, Pittenweem 58, St Monans 104, Largo 18, Buckhaven 120, Crail 5, St Andrews 11, total 489.

Montrose and Stonehaven were the ports again. By August, one hundred and forty boats were fishing from Anstruther. Little doing, and only 4,000 crans landed in Anstruther all summer, the District being 15,000 crans compared with 31,000 the previous year.

1866

This was to be a very important year in the District, mainly for Anstruther and Cellardyke, for it saw the beginning of the building of the east pier at

Anstruther which had been long talked about. Most of the fishermen lived in Cellardyke so they wanted the harbour to be at Craig Noon, a rock formation at Cellardyke, which would have given them a deep water harbour. Anstruther being a town of business people wanted it developed west of the present inner harbour at Anstruther, and, as their finances were better, the decision was made to develop Anstruther harbour rather than to build a new deep water harbour. However, as it was not built in a day, it will be mentioned in more detail as developments occurred.

Rough weather in January saw little fishing in the mouth of the Firth, but large takes were got between Inchkeith and Aberdour, and sixty boats one day landed an average of 8 crans at 3s. per 100 in Newhaven. The crews are mentioned as being 3-5 men per boat. The boats were going twice to sea in one day, first in the afternoon and again about 11 p.m. It was an open winter, with little snow before the middle of February, but it was very stormy. The fishing was very poor until the last week of February, and there was poverty, but the able-bodied poor were not entitled to relief. Two English luggers had heavy catches of cod and ling, and a large shoal of herring set in at the mouth of the Firth, and on Wednesday, February 20th, one hundred and forty-five boats landed 1,160 crans in Anstruther, prices 23s. One boat lost 27 nets, as they were too full of fish. Thirty of the local boats went into Crail. Stormy weather with a heavy ground swell then brought the fishing to a conclusion, with only 5,630 crans and 10,000 for the District.

The small lines were again the saviour of the coast, and great haddock catches were made from April to the end of June.

Meanwhile preparations were afoot for the start of the building of the Anstruther East Pier. and a great deal of quarrying took place at Craighead Farm, Crail by a large group of men, and by the end of April as much had been quarried as would do a fourth part of the pier. The experts were well pleased with the stone, and thought it would weather well, (and so it has, as you can see today at the back of the east pier). There was no through road at that time, past the head of the east pier, and a line of rails was run from the head of the present middle pier to the scene of the operations opposite the gasworks, where old houses were removed.

During this time, a meeting took place of two men who had been boys together at Crieffie's 'schule abune the braes' (Moncrieff's School opposite the head of the wee wynd in Cellardyke). They were Captain Alex Rodger, master of the China Tea Clippers *Kate Carnie* and *Ellen Rodger,* and owner of the *Min, Taeping* and *Lahloo,* and Sir Walter Hughes, home from Australia, owner of rich copper mines and founder of Adelaide University. Rodger, a native of

Crail harbour. The *Comely,* ML 360, with a shot of 26 crans from the anchor nets in the Auld Haikes. The crew were J. Watson, W. Smith, T. Meldrum, H. Smith and his father, W. Smith. She was built in Leith in 1901 as a pilot boat then sold to D. & A. Deas of Buckhaven as a fishing boat. Jock Deas of Cellardyke bought her in the mid-1920s and when the author's father was one of the crew they filled her twice in one day from the Mill Bay, to the east of Cellardyke. In 1933 Harry Smith of Crail bought her and in 1936 they filled her three times in one day from their anchored nets in the Auld Haikes.

Cellardyke, and Hughes, a native of Pittenweem, had both spent some of their youth as East Fife fishermen. They were greatly interested in the building of the new harbour, and Hughes had a fishing boat built about 60 ft. long with a fore and aft rig, and on July 13th his boat, the *Pioneer,* was launched. Although she was fast and did not require to lower the sail each time she tacked as the Fifies did, they reckoned she could not sail as close to the wind as they did, so she did not catch on, and had to be sold. This was a pity, as the lug sail was to be the cause of the drowning of many men, due to this awkward manoeuvre while tacking. In passing, it is interesting to note that Sir Walter Hughes left the fishing to sail to the whaling, with the *William and Ann* of Leith, with another classmate, Captain Smith of whale's jawbone fame.

Most of the boats spent the summer at Montrose and Stonehaven and some fished well there, and not until the last week of August did any number fish in the Firth, the best day seeing one hundred boats average 18 crans in Anstruther, prices 23s.-27s., but all from the White Spot. The season's figures were only 4,000 crans in Anstruther, Pittenweem 1,600, St Monans 2,600, District 8,000.

On September 14th the Tea Clipper Race ended when *Taeping* and *Ariel* arrived at London, *Taeping* being declared the winner, although the *Ariel,* with Master John Keay of Anstruther Wester, took on her pilot first, but the tide being out, both ships had to await the rising tide, and the *Taeping,* having the lighter cargo, was able to enter London docks first, twenty minutes before the *Ariel.* So that the bounty given to the winner should not be lost, it was agreed that the *Taeping* was the winner, although the prize money was shared. The Master of the *Taeping* was Captain McKinnon of Tiree, and the owner Captain Rodger of Cellardyke, later of Glasgow. This caused much excitement locally, and I have heard it mentioned that there were Dykers in the *Taeping's* crew, and Anstruther men in the *Ariel's.* Certainly a Fowler and a Watson were in the *Taeping,* but I have never heard of any local people claiming to be with Captain John Keay in the *Ariel.*

To conclude this memorable year, ten or twelve boats prepared to go to the autumn fishing at Yarmouth, among them Peter Murray in the *Carmi* in her first year. He also seems to have owned the *Choice,* the first local boat to be half-decked, but as the *Carmi* was able to go to Yarmouth, we must assume that the bigger local boats were now fully decked.

By the end of the year, the outer wall of the new east pier had been built out to a distance of 100 yards, but the Rowin stanes were not sufficient for packing between the walls of the pier.

1867

Most of the winter months were spent packing between the walls of the pier, and a great deal of quarrying went ahead at the Billowness, where the stone unfortunately did not prove to weather as well as the Crail stone, so it was just used for packing. By the middle of January the new steamer *Forth* arrived for the new Steam Shipping Company. It cost £1,500. Severe storms in January confined most of the fishing to the upper reaches of the Firth, and some of the boats ran to Elie for shelter. By the beginning of February, some of the local boats had decided to go to the great lines, because of lack of herring, yet a large number of English buyers had appeared. During the first week of February, herring appeared close to the shore at Kirkcaldy and people anchored pieces of net on the beach at low water, getting a goodly number of herrings in them on the next tide, prices 40s. per barrel.

As the weather improved, seventy-six boats operated from Anstruther, and the fishing gradually improved so that on Saturday, 14th February, eighty-five boats landed 720 crans in Anstruther, prices 22s.-30s. Pittenweem and St Monans were also well fished, and the railway was blamed for not having enough trucks available. Large catches of cod were also landed, some by English luggers, and on February 27th, one hundred and thirty-five boats landed 1,020 crans in Anstruther, prices 9s.-12s. 6d., which was the first time in 17 years that the price had gone below 10s. 8,690 crans were landed in Anstruther for the season and 18,000 for the District, the best since 1861. At the beginning of April the *Pioneer* landed the largest catch of white fish in Anstruther by one vessel, valued at more than £50. Meanwhile the new East Pier of Anstruther harbour had been making steady progress. Both the outer and inner walls were carried on simultaneously with a line of rails inside, and by mid-April 150 yards of the outer wall had been completed. Trucks were drawn on rails from the inner basin by horses, and 150 men were employed overall.

By May, half the local boats were at the great lines, and the rest at the small lines.

Haddocks fetched 9s.-11s. per 100, halibut 3s. 9d.-4s. 6d. per stone, ling 1s. 3d.-1s. 9d. each, cod 9d. each. By the beginning of June, the Buckhaven men had left for the Tyne fishing. (This fishing was opened up two years previously by the Fife fishermen and it was reported that one hundred sail was expected, from as far away as Lowestoft.)

By the end of June some of the local boats stayed ashore to bark their nets. (As this is the first mention of barking nets, it seems that the nets were now mainly cotton and the hemp nets had died out.) After a good line fishing season, one hundred and fifty boats from Anstruther and Cellardyke prosecuted the herring fishing from Peterhead and Fraserburgh, coming south to Montrose and Gourdon towards the end of July. By August, twenty of the local boats fished from Anstruther but herring were near the Bell Rock, and only in the second last week of August did a shoal set in at the Auld Haikes. On August 21st eighty boats landed 1,130 crans in Anstruther at 20s.-24s. per cran.

St Monans was the best fished port in the District, eighty boats averaging 15 crans in one day. An old adage of 'Haikes herring', 'sure of a basketful, sure of a boat load', no longer appeared to be true. 7,000 crans was Anstruther's total for the season, 21,900 for the District, with St Monans the best with 8,960, the first time since records began that the port had beaten Anstruther and Cellardyke.

October 4th saw the launch of a new boat, *Scotch Lassie,* by Bailie Pottinger. All decked, 45 ft. by 16 ft. by 7ft., the skipper was R. Brown and it was owned

Anstruther harbour in the early 1920s, before the bauldies had wheelhouses. In the foreground are the bauldies *Refuge, Enterprise,* and *Fisher Lassie,* with the steam drifter *Scot* behind them. The *Enterprise* was the first boat in which the author went to the winter herring, at the age of nine.

by R.N.L.I. Since the end of the summer fishing a great many of the large line boats had become fully decked. No mention was made of Yarmouth, but the small line fishing remained poor for the rest of the year. New harbour works reached low water mark but a violent storm caused some damage, but nothing like the trouble that was to come.

1868

There was still no telegraph between Anstruther and Thornton, and this was blamed for the lateness on the part of the Coastguards in hoisting north or south cones as gale warnings. January was a very stormy month with mention of a hurricane south south-west in the last week. There were poor fishings in all the local ports and even near the end of February the tale was one of a succession of westerly gales. The best day of the season was March 2nd, when one hundred and forty boats landed 920 crans in Anstruther, prices 9s.-20s. per cran. Pittenweem and St Monans were also very good. However, March proved to be quite a good month and the season finished with Anstruther totalling 10,760 crans, the best year since 1861.

About this time, there appeared in the town a boy in a velvet jacket, and a plaque on a house just north of East Anstruther Kirk commemorates the stay of

R.L. Stevenson in Anstruther. His visit is recounted in his book of essays *Across the Plains.*

With the recurring failure of the local summer fishing, most of the boats now fished north during July and August and the best day locally was August 11th, when one hundred and ten boats landed 1,045 crans in Anstruther from the Bell Rock area, prices 22s.6d-24s.6d. During the two months only 6,000 crans were landed in Anstruther. Pittenweem and St Monans fared worse as most of the herring were in the Bell Rock area. Only 13,000 crans were landed for the District. Again there was no word of boats going to Yarmouth or Lowestoft. A violent storm in mid-September caused great destruction of the harbour works, mainly to the staging and diving apparatus. The storm lasted for more than 48 hours. The high sea wall of the outer section on which three months' labour had been spent was completely overthrown from the bight, and underneath the rubble lay the diving bell.

1869

Four Buckie boats arrived in January for winter herring. January had open weather with the mention of a typical local storm.

January 27th—There was a severe south-easterly gale veering westerly but it soon passed. Herring fishing was poor at local ports but many cod were caught by hand lines. Only one February day saw a large catch.

February 3rd—One hundred and forty boats landed 1,250 crans in Anstruther, prices 30s.-35s. Pittenweem and St Monans also well fished that week. (An article in the *East Fife Record* at that time reported that before the coming of the railways to Edinburgh, the winter herring was prosecuted mainly by old men and boys, for bait for the sea-going fleet. Anything over was bought and cured for the West Indian market and ships in Pittenweem made up their cargo with the surplus. The herring were sold for feeding the slaves in Tobago, but they cured as 'dry as sticks'. The fishing was made by English buyers coming up to Edinburgh by train and down from Leith in the packet boat. The surplus herring were turned into Yarmouth bloaters.) February had westerly gales all month and the first week in March saw the first fall of snow of the winter.

Mr Addy, the fish buyer whose name is stamped on the salesman's bell which is in the local Fishermen's Museum in Anstruther, was mentioned with George Thomson as one of the men who raised the price of lobsters and one dozen partans to 1s. and 1s.6d respectively, prices which remained constant for the next sixty to seventy years. The previous year, 1868, was mentioned as the poorest general year since 1834 although, strangely enough, Peterhead and Fraserburgh had good fishings in both years. The winter herring closed with 8,000 crans in Anstruther for the year and about 13,000 for the District. Most of the boats went north for the summer fishing, but in mid-August a shoal set in, in the Traith where the St Monans men fished quite well for the rest of the month. Only 3,000 crans were landed in Anstruther that summer, the lowest up to that time; St Monans had nearly 5,000 and the District 10,800.

Work continued on the building of the east pier. The staging which had been washed down in the storm the previous year was re-erected, and the roadway was causewayed with Carlingnose blocks 24″ by 14″ laid on a bed of concrete. The upper mooring pauls were made of Carlingnose blue whinstone, the lower ones of cast iron with perforated heads. This part of the pier was also bound together by strong iron bands. By June only 100 ft of the pier remained to be built. The western breakwater was not to be proceeded with as the loan was almost exhausted.

1870

Most of the winter was spent at the small line fishing where Peter Murray spent his first winter in his new boat *Venus*, not having gone south to Lowestoft since 1866. As many as forty-two boats were fishing during the winter line fishing from Anstruther and Cellardyke. Catches were as high as 36cwts of haddocks per shot, price 14s. per cwt. By the end of January, the number of local boats at the winter herring were given as Anstruther and Cellardyke seventy, Pittenweem eighteen, St Monans forty-three, Elie two, Largo eight, Buckhaven fifty-six. However, it was to be the lowest winter herring season on record apart from 1864, accompanied by high prices of 40s.-50s. because of the scarcity. Total for the season was 4,165 crans for Anstruther and 6,600 for the District.

At the beginning of February, the east pier was struck by a violent storm lasting four to five days. A breach of seventy to eighty feet was made in the parapet wall, allowing the sea through to bring down the quay wall. A round parapet at the point remained, like a sentinel beacon beside the ragged wall facing it on the east. Later in the month another storm extended the gap to ninety feet. Contractors were given instructions to build up the face of the wall eighty yards from the point as the end of the pier, and remove the rounded point which had withstood the storm.

Launch of the *Pursuit*, KY 152, by Miller at St Monans in 1926.

Kingsbarns harbour was built about this time by Thomas Duncan of Boghall, who used it for shipping potatoes. In ten years it was to be the property of Sir Thomas Erskine.

James Watson of Pittenweem started to build houses fronting the railway station viz. Watson Place.

By June, the line fishing which had been fairly good appeared to be finished and Sharp and Murray, fish buyers of Cellardyke, engaged nine local boats at 20s. per cran and £10 bounty either at Anstruther, Gourdon or Stonehaven. By mid-July the Buckhaven boats returned from Shields. William Easson's boat gained upwards of £230.

By mid-July war was declared between France and Russia, an event which was likely to upset the markets. Bread rose in price from 7d. to 8d. July 26th saw telegraphic communications established at the Post Office and the railway station. Two wires existed between Anstruther and Thornton, one exclusively for the railway, but the other coastal towns were not yet connected. By the end of July the curers had paid their engaged boats their bounty and so disengaged themselves because of the war.

Anstruther harbour, with the crews of the local drifters *Lasher, Cassiopeia,* and *Spes Melior* setting up their nets.

A Cellardyke man was fined 11s. for smuggling 2½ lb of foreign tobacco. Fishing was good north at Peterhead and Fraserburgh, and attracted local boats away, so local landings were mainly due to men coming home for weekends. Only twenty to thirty boats remained during the week and St Monans and Buckhaven men who remained in the Firth were nearly in debt.

St Monans boats who fished north all did well, but the trawling they had done in the Treath in previous years was blamed for the failure of the local Lammas fishing which hit Pittenweem harder than the other local ports. This year saw *Tarry* mentioned for the first time for barking the nets.

By the end of September, twenty-five to thirty local boats were preparing for the autumn fishing. Although they were going south, they probably did not go further than Scarborough. By December local boats returned from the south with good fishings ranging from £200-£370.

As for the harbour, an October storm washed down a great portion of what was to have been the point of the pier and a December storm caused more cracks in the outer wall which was believed to oscillate ½" with each wave.

1871 and 1872

These years are grouped together as they represented a new peak in the winter herring fishing, accompanied by a decline in the local Lammas fishing.

In January 1871, Buckhaven enjoyed a month of almost unprecedented success and good fishing was enjoyed up the Firth before the herring set in locally in February. Unfortunately, easterly gales set in and Elie must have presented an unusual sight as one hundred and fifty boats sheltered there in the first week of February. In Anstruther on February 13th, one hundred and twelve boats landed 900 crans at 30s.-38s. per cran, fishing near May Island.

In the first week in March, a boat went ashore on the Ghats, the large skelly to the west of Anstruther harbour, which was the gateway to the old harbour. Several boats used the new harbour for the first time but the roadway was not suitable for carts.

March 1st saw one hundred and forty-three boats land 1,287 crans at 13s.-21s. in Anstruther.

Over 12,000 crans were landed in Anstruther for the season and 24,000 for the District. Most of the local boats fished in the north now, with Aberdeen being mentioned, and the local summer fishing totalled only 1,900 crans. A contemporary article gives the cran measure as 37½ imperial gallons with one barrel equalling 26⅔ imperial gallons, but after being cured and 'pined', one cran is approximately one barrel. The financing of the new pier was raised in Parliament and a further £6,000 was granted to make and deposit large blocks of concrete to protect the damaged part of the east pier. An October storm, however, did further damage, and concrete had to be used to fill up the cracks in the pier and in thirty of the large blocks laid at the back of the pier, and so the money ran out again.

1872

Another good winter herring fishing saw a peak in the first week of March with two successive one day totals exceeding 1,500 crans, one hundred and sixty boats being the maximum recorded. The total this year was 11,000 crans for Anstruther and 21,000 for the District. Prices collapsed to 2s. 6d a cran on these peak days. Five hundred boats were engaged at Montrose for the summer fishing.

Local boats fished mainly at Aberdeen, Stonehaven and Montrose. Very few boats fished locally, twenty-four being the highest number mentioned. Only 1,800 crans were landed in Anstruther for the summer, with only 3,000 for the District. Most of the boats seemed to be employed at the small lines. As for the harbour, work came to a standstill when the grant was all spent. Mr Ellice, the M.P. for St Andrews Burghs, managed to get the Chancellor of the

Exchequer to inspect the new harbour works when on a visit to St Andrews, and this produced a further enquiry in the House of Commons.

1873

Mixed fortunes locally for the local fishings. On January 17th 1873 the winter lines produced 320 tons of haddocks. It was a very poor winter herring fishing, stormy and with few shoals.

The maximum number of boats was one hundred and fifty, and the maximum catch for a day was 550 crans, producing a low total of 4,000 crans in Anstruther and 9,000 for the District. By the end of March, the prices reached as high as £10 for a cran.

By the end of June, Bonthron had auctioned 13,000 halibut, 18,000 ling, 14,000 skate, 28,000 small codlins, 146,000 cod, 17,000 saithe etc.

Eyemouth, which had its first decked boat built in 1856, 40 ft. long and costing £130, now had forty fully decked boats of 44-50 ft. long, while Buckie had four hundred fully decked boats.

The summer fishing had been quite good north but only 2,000 crans were landed in Anstruther and 4,000 for the District. The Government had voted another £9,000 for the harbour and it was decided to finish the east pier to the original length using concrete, and this stands to this day. From the end of the parapet westwards to the point, it was completely made of concrete. This so angered the masons, that they condemned it as 'nothing but putty', and as the west breakwater was made entirely of concrete it got the local name of the 'Potty Pier'.

It was decided that the west breakwater was to be built of concrete at a width of 21 feet (which it remained until the major reconstruction of the 1930s). To protect the old harbour, cement blocks were to be laid at the back of the west pier, as well as the east pier. In the spring, the ground at the Billowness from Johnny Doo's pulpit inwards, which had been broken up by the quarrying, was harrowed and seeded with grass (and if you look carefully today you will see that it is a coarse, hay type of grass, not the bent sea grasses which can be seen further west).

1874

This was the last good winter herring fishing for some time. February was the best month of a mild winter, the best day being February 18th, when one

A Fifie bauldie being launched from Aitken's yard at Anstruther in the 1930s. He built
many similar models both for local skippers and for owners from N.E. England. All were
about 50ft in length. They were built in a yard on the landward side of the main road
and the day before the launch the road was closed while a slipway was built across it and
the boat was dragged across until she was poised ready to take the water.

hundred and forty boats landed 1,250 crans, prices 7s. 6d.-11s. By the middle of
March the season was over, 11,000 crans in Anstruther and 20,000 for the
District. Most of the local boats now went north for the summer fishing,
including St Monans and Pittenweem boats, so only yawls were left to fish
locally for the Lammas Drave. There were seven hundred and eighty-seven
boats in the District employing over 7,000 men and boys. Local boats did well
north, the best fisher being Peter Murray in the *Venus*. That year the Marquis
of Tweeddale gave twenty sea thermometers to the Fishery Officers; (the only
one in Anstruther was given to my grandfather, P. Smith who, with his
brother Willie, had a boat *True Love*) and 55°F two miles off Anstruther, 56 °F
east of the Bell Rock, 54°F off Eyemouth were the recorded readings. The
summer fishing in Anstruther produced only 1,000 crans, less than 2,000 for the
District.

  The west pier was completed by the end of June, and the cut mouth stands to
the present day. The old parapet wall was pulled down (except for that part of
the west pier from the steps in the wall to the cut mouth) and so the harbour
appears to have been completed except for the old harbour mouth which was
still open.

1875

Two mediocre years locally were redeemed only by good summer fishings in the north. Many of the crews continued at the haddock lines instead of the winter herring in 1875, which seems to have been a stormy winter. The best day was February 9th when one hundred and twenty-four boats landed 1,130 crans at 20s.-29s. The season saw 6,000 crans landed in Anstruther, 8,000 for the District. By the middle of March, many boats had gone to the great line fishing. Many more yawls prosecuted the partan fishing, as the previous year had produced the best returns ever. In England the limit was said to be 4½″, which it was up to the Second World War. Here, there was still no limit to the size, and small partans were sold at 6d. per dozen and large ones at 2s. per dozen. One merchant sent 300 dozen to the English markets from Anstruther in one week. The Buckland enquiry into the herring fishing in England, suggested a close time until the end of May and the restriction of the maximum number of meshes to 30-36 per yard. Pittenweem men were at Howth and Kinsale in June. One hundred and sixty-six Cellardyke boats went north in July. The Scotch Fishery Board report for 1874 recorded that it was the first year in which 1,000,000 barrels were cured. So few boats were left locally during the summer that only 250 crans were landed in Anstruther and 280 in the District. The Cellardyke boats did well in the north. Andrew Henderson was the best with £400. As for the harbour works, sixty Cellardyke fishermen signed a letter composed by Captain Rodger, complaining about the two mouths to the harbour.

1876

A poor winter herring saw high prices, seldom below £2 all season. 3,000 crans were landed in Anstruther, 5,000 for the District. Anstruther totalled only 100 crans for the summer and the District 170. J. Brunton did well north with £400, the best this year. Peter Murray in the *Venus* was at Stornoway from May to June, then Peterhead in July and August, and spent the winter from October to February at the haddock lines. The gradual development of the Summer Drave in the north led to it becoming the major fishing area. The harbour was completed as it was to stand until the 1930s. By the end of August, men had started to block up the old harbour entrance and by December the bridge over the cut mouth had been removed, the old harbour mouth closed, and a temporary bridge placed over it pending the laying of a roadway.

1877

During the worst winter herring fishing since records began, Tom Brown, the English fish buyer, cured 38 tons of haddocks, and to the end of the winter herrings Tom Brown's firm still came to Anstruther from England.

Only 1,400 crans were landed in Anstruther, St Monans 600, Buckhaven 300, the District 2,500.

February saw the Leading Lights erected at the New Harbour and June saw the death of Captain Rodger. During the summer most of the local boats fished in the north and one boat, having 100 crans, sent a message ashore to Aberdeen by carrier pigeon for a tug to tow her in. 1,500 crans were landed in Anstruther for the summer. These were poor times locally and Peter Murray of the *Venus* went to Lowestoft in October and November, the first time for ten years.

1878

A slight recovery in the winter herring fishing was accompanied by a long period of good weather. The last week of February saw ninety to one hundred and thirty boats landing totals of 700-800 crans in a day. A new boat of 48½ feet was built for James Smith (Lowpie) which is a timely reminder that the biggest boats at that time were only about 40 feet long. It was reported that D. Allan of Granton had built two steam drifters, the *Forward* for Methven of Leith and the *Onward* for Sharp and Murray of Cellardyke. The latter was unable to get a Cellardyke crew for her so she fished from Aberdeen. It was to be a further four years before the first steam trawler fished from there. 6,000 crans were landed in Anstruther for the season. Some local boats were engaged to Sharp and Murray for the summer at Montrose, Gourdon etc. and a steam tug, *Perthshire,* was hired to tow their boats.

Only seven or eight boats fished the summer herring from Anstruther, and they totalled 1,500 crans, 3,900 for the District. In the north, Fraserburgh and Peterhead had good seasons, but not the Montrose area, and Adam Watson was reckoned to be King of the Fishers.

The *Venus Star* was launched for Peter Murray and many old boats were sold to England and replaced by new boats.

1879

Alum for treating the nets was in general use this year, but poor fishings continued. Mr Atkins, a local fishbuyer, engaged 12 out of the 24 local crews

Anstruther harbour with the Pittenweem boat *Seton Castle,* KY 64, in the foreground.
Behind her are the local steam drifters *Spes Melior, Spes Aurea,* and the *Sunny Bird* of
Peterhead. In the background is the bauldie *Ben Venuto,* AH 44.

who were at the creels at 1s. 9d. per dozen for crabs, (more than we got in the
1930s), and 1s. each for lobsters. by the middle of February, prospects were so
poor that many of the boats reverted to the lines. Only 1,500 crans were landed
in Anstruther for the season, and 2,000 for the District. Even the great line
fishing was poor. The damage to the fishing by steam trawling in the Firth was
a matter of much speculation. At the end of August a shoal set in close to the
shore west of the Billowness, and all the yawls with old nets were used by local
tradesmen; one yawl making £100 in one week. Curing was done on the Folly
for the first time for years. The herring also set in the Haikes, where a yawl
sank due to the weight of the herring and eighteen boats landed 1,000 in one day
in Anstruther, prices 20s.-22s., 5,000 crans for the season, and 6,000 for the
District.

1880

Although not much evidence of it was seen this year the winter herring
fishing was about to expand. A buoy had been fixed to the south-west of

Anstruther harbour, and Captain James Henderson of *S.S. Anna* took a rope from the pier to the buoy so that if the winds were adverse the local sailing vessels could use it at the cost of 1s. a time. By the beginning of March one hundred and forty boats were at the local fishing and the total for the season was 5,000 crans, 8,000 for the District. March saw the inauguration of Chalmers Memorial Lighthouse.

By July, one hundred and eighty Cellardyke and Anstruther boats were at the Drave at Montrose or further north. Large shoals appeared off the Forfarshire and Kincardineshire coasts. Among the areas mentioned were White Spat, Cockenzie Reef and Kilrenny Reef. One hundred cran shot was dumped at Stonehaven. Four thousand crans were landed locally mainly at weekends as the local boats came home from the Montrose area. For the District the total was 7,000. As the local Lammas fishing began to die, the winter herring began to flourish. Even though the locals fished at many different places during the summer and (apart from the small lines) only at home during the winter, only the records of the winter fishing are actually significant.

1881

By the end of January, the winter herring fishing was general from an area about the May Island. There were two days without frost in January. On January 26th, one hundred and fifty-five boats landed 270 crans in Anstruther, prices 39s.–44s. 6d. At the beginning of February, the herring set in close to the shore, and on February 16th, one hundred and seventy boats landed 800 crans in Anstruther, 38s.–43s. Prices remained good throughout February as there were few herrings landed elsewhere. Storms interrupted the fishing in March but over 11,000 crans were landed in Anstruther for the season, nearly 17,000 for the District. It was the most valuable winter herring on record, as the prices seldom fell below 30s. per cran. The local boats had all but deserted the Forth during the summer although a fleet of nearly one hundred boats pursued a summer fishing out of Dunbar. Usually the weekend was the main landing time for the local boats as they came home occasionally from Montrose. The local boats which had gone to Peterhead and Fraserburgh did well, and this appeared now to be the most remunerative fishing. In the autumn some of the bigger boats went south, mainly at this time to Scarborough as few of the boats were as long as 50 ft.

1882

By the end of January, the herring were inshore and fishing was better in the west and by February 7th, two hundred boats had landed 800 crans in Anstruther, prices 30s.-35s. February saw much the same area for the fishing, and all season the Buckhaven boats were best fished, as the smaller boats were better able to cope with the inshore herring. It had been an open winter as the first real snow fall only came in March. During that month, two 50 ft. boats were launched for John Gardner and James Barclay (two well-known Cellardyke names). One of the north boats went home by the middle of March having grossed £200. It had been a season of westerly winds and the Anstruther landings exceeded 9,000 crans, the District 13,000. Two interesting pieces of news appeared in June. Jarvis was building the largest boat in the District for David Wilson, and the N.L.I. was offering cheap aneroid barometers to the fishermen. It was obvious the prospects locally for the fishermen were good and a list of men having boats launched was given, nine by Jarvis and six by Miller.

1881	October 8	W Wood (Pittenweem)	50 ft.
	December 8	R Brown (Cellardyke)	51½ ft.
1882	January 21	G Watson (Cellardyke)	50 ft.
	February 20	J Brown (Cellardyke)	52 ft.
	February 20	Jas. Smith (Brown) (Cellardyke)	50½ ft.
	March 6	J Gardner (Cellardyke)	50 ft.
	March 6	J & J Barclay (Cellardyke)	50 ft.
	March 21	M Gardner (Cellardyke)	54 ft.
	April 4	D Gore (Gourdon)	47 ft.
	April 20	W Cormack (.Wick)	45 ft.
	June 3	J & J Muir (Cellardyke)	51 ft.
	June 17	W Reid (Wood) (Cellardyke)	50½ ft.
	June 17	J Stewart (Stevenson) (Cellardyke)	46 ft.
	June 17	G Moncrieff (Watson) (Cellardyke)	47 ft.
	July 4	D Wilson (Cellardyke)	54½ ft.

The summer fishing had developed a pattern now of the big boats all fishing in the north, leaving only a few yawls to fish at home. The local landings were about the same as the previous year, about 2,000 crans. Again the local boats had a good summer fishing but a poor Scarborough one in the autumn.

1883

This was a year similar to the previous one with a good winter herring totalling about 9,000 crans in Anstruther and over 13,000 for the District. With the continued growth of the winter herring fishing, the pattern for the year seemed to be as follows: the winter herring from January to March, followed by great lines from April to June, north fishing for herring in July to September, south, either to Scarborough or Lowestoft, in October and November, followed by the haddock lines during the winter period before the start of the winter herring. The most remunerative fishing at this time seems to have been the Summer Drave, July to September, in the north, which often was more than half of the total year's earnings. It was natural that boats should go where there were good markets and that was no longer in the Forth ports.

1884

The first week of February saw two days with totals exceeding 2,000 crans landed in Anstruther from one hundred and thirty to one hundred and sixty boats. This brought the prices down to 7s. 6d. a cran, lower than for the two pervious seasons and on February 23rd, one hundred and ninety boats landed 1,500 crans in Anstruther, prices 17s.-18s. 6d.

This was the greatest winter herring up to that time, 22,000 crans for the season in Anstruther, and 33,000 for the District. In June many of the Cellardyke boats left for Shetland but they soon returned to Fraserburgh or Peterhead. In total two hundred boats went north from Anstruther and Cellardyke. Jarvis was still busy at the boat building yard and in the year he launched fifteen fishing boats and one steam trawler, 104 ft. long, for Montrose. Nine of the boats were from 51-58 ft. and six from 20-30 ft. John Linn was supposed to finish the last block at the back of the east pier in July. There were again successful fishings in the north, one local boat grossing over £300. Scarborough fishing, however, was poor.

1885

Because of the previous good winter herring fishing, forty stranger boats arrived by the middle of January and by the end of January, unusually early, good catches were obtained. January 19th, one hundred and forty-three boats

The *Ivy*, KY 68, entering Anstruther harbour. The sail is on the back of the mast with the tack to the 'Stellum', and the author is at the tiller. This is the last boat in which he hauled a winter herring net.

had 1,150 crans, prices 15s.-32s. January 20th, one hundred and fifty boats had 2,000 crans, 6s.-10s. per cran. January 21st, one hundred and fifteen boats had 1,000 crans, 7s.-8s.

Because of the collapse of the prices some crews stayed ashore and on Tuesday 26th, one hundred and fifty boats landed 3,500 crans at 4s.-5s. per cran—the greatest day ever at the winter herring (not exceeded even in the 1930s). The railway dispatched 280 waggons loaded with herring that day. Although we do not have full details of what happened at Pittenweem and St Monans, it is known that most of the Pittenweem catch went for bloaters. 1,800 crans were landed on Friday 29th January, but prices slumped to 2s. 6d. the cran.

Because of the low prices, February saw general fishing from fewer boats, as many started the great line fishing early. By March, most of the herring was sold for bait and the season's total surpassed the previous years and established a new record of 25,000 crans in Anstruther and 36,000 crans for the District.

The great line prices were interesting as cod only fetched 1s. 6d.-1s. 9d. while ling were sold for double that price. The local boats finished with the great lines about the beginning of June when thirty boats left for Shetland. The great line fishing had been less than average. Kinsale had been a failure and the locals were unlikely to go again. By the first week in July, two Cellardyke boats, those of J. Watson and J. Brunton, had completed their complements of 160 crans at Shetland. By mid-July, two hundred boats had left for the Drave mainly at Aberdeen. From Anstruther only seven or eight boats prosecuted the herring fishing along with some Pittenweem boats, but only a few crans were landed, and complaints were made about trawlers operating in the Traith. The summer fishing was only average, with Shetland being the most successful. After a good autumn fishing at Yarmouth and Lowestoft the previous year, several local boats attempted that long journey again but had only moderate success.

1886

Mild weather in autumn and early winter in Scandinavia resulted in a serious depression, a portent of things to come. Even in the first week of January, Norwegian herrings were selling in London at 5s. per cran; yet the railway carriage from Anstruther to London was 15s. per cran. By the middle of January, between four and five thousand crans of Norwegian herrings were reported in London, and the prices of herring in Anstruther in January seldom exceeded £1 per cran. In the last week of January, one hundred and eight boats landed 1,200 crans in Anstruther, prices 6s.-9s. per cran. At the beginning of February two reasons were being given for the poor prices, Norwegian herring in London and a very depressed state of trade in the country. In the second week of February, four successive days saw totals in Anstruther exceeding 1,000 crans and on February 12th, one hundred and thirty-three boats landed 2,000 crans at 2s. per cran. These depressed prices saw several boats giving up the herring fishing for the great lines, and on February 26th, the largest boat locally was built for James Smith (Watson), 58½ ft., but this record did not last as long as a month because James Reekie, St Monans, launched for James Bowman (Pittenweem), a boat of length 61 ft. At the end of March, another 56 ft. boat the *James Ritchie Welch,* KY393, was launched at Anstruther. (It was unusual to give both the name and number at this time.) About this time, Messrs. Duncan & Black of Cellardyke made successful experiments with a new patent canvas buoy in the presence of Cellardyke and Buckhaven fishermen. Whereas the dogskin supported a weight of 70 lbs, the new canvas buoy supported a weight of 90 lbs.

Meanwhile, a new bye-law was passed prohibiting trawling west of a line from Fife Ness to St Abbs Head. During the year, the May Island got a new light of four flashes (this was not altered until 1924). The winter herring fishing had been pursued by two hundred and twenty boats landing 18,000 crans in Anstruther and 25,000 crans in the District. Never again in the nineteenth century were two hundred boats engaged at the winter herring because of the poor prices of 1886, thanks to the Norwegians. This summer saw the ending of the bounty and engagement system and although many more local boats had been tempted to fish at Shetland, they were not as successful as the previous year. Altogether this was a very poor year for the local fishing boats. 6,000 crans were landed locally during the summer, as several boats came home early from the north. The Scarborough fishing was also down.

1887

Prices stood up better in the first fortnight of January and on the 19th of January, one hundred and twelve boats landed a total of 350 crans, prices 24s.-32s. per cran.

The *Golden Rule,* KY 335, belonging to George Keay was run down this side of Fidra by the Cockenzie boat *Shimri* and by the end of January, there was a claim that the new electric light of four flashes from the May Island, had been observed 46 miles at sea. The abolition of the Beam Trawl resulted in 100 boxes of plaice being caught by line in St Andrews Bay.

Prices were soon to fall, however, due to the import of Norwegian herring. Despite 500 telegrams passing through Anstruther Post Office, the prices did not recover, and on February 10th, one hundred and forty-five boats landed 1,300 crans, prices 5s.-6s. per cran. There was no lack of herring, although the fleet was drastically reduced, and from the middle of February to the middle of March there were many days of good fishing, one of the best being March 1st, when one hundred and forty-six boats landed 1,500 crans, prices only 2s. 6d.-4s. On March 8th fifty-five boats landed 850 crans, prices 2s. 6d.-8s. 9d., with the *Venus Star* having 82 crans. By this time twenty-eight of the bigger local boats had given up the herring fishing because of the poor prices and were pursuing the great line fishing.

An official cran measure was sent to each Fishery Officer by the Fishery Board (1 cran = 40 gallons or 37 ½ imperial gallons), and the winter herring just faded away without any real increase in price. Poor financially, the depleted fleet of one hundred and seventy-six maximum landed 32,000 crans for the District and 25,000 in Anstruther. A great storm in April saw much damage and loss of life. Also in April, the wheel for steering instead of the 'tully' was mentioned for the first time. The great line fishing alone saved the fleet this year as the summer fishing was a failure and at the end of August, although there was plenty of herring, four hundred of the local boats averaged only between £80 and £90 gross due to bad prices.

At the end of September the loom in the sky of the four flashes of the May Light were seen 56 miles out at sea and Fulton had built a 60 ft. boat for Stonehaven with a capstan. Scarborough was a failure, one boat sharing out only 9s. per man, but Yarmouth and Lowestoft were better. Although the Yarmouth and Lowestoft fishing was not well documented, there were some two hundred and fifty Scots boats in this area and they averaged £100 to £200 gross each. By the end of November all the Scots boats were home, one Cellardyke boat, *Lavinia,* skipper David Birrell, setting a record of 32 hours for the journey home. One who did not return was James Brunton who was drowned at Yarmouth.

1888

One hundred and thirty boats were actively engaged in the herring fishing by the middle of January, but prices soon fell, the recurring theme for a few years to come, and by February 2nd, one hundred and sixty-four boats landed a total of 1,310 crans, prices 9s.-11s. per cran. The low prices forced thirty crews to give up and start the great lines, and on February 23rd, one hundred and four boats landed 1,200 crans, prices 8s.-13s. Poor weather and a glut of herring at other ports reduced prices to 1s. a cran, bought for manure. Although a rough March of east winds and snow reduced the catches, 25,000 crans were landed in the District from one hundred and eighty-eight boats, 20,000 in Anstruther. The average price was 9s. 7d. per cran, compared with 8s. the previous year. The new lifeboat, the *Royal Stewart,* arrived in May, and she was capsized and righted herself after her christening. During the summer more boats fished at home than for several years, but without much success, only 2,000 crans for the season. Three hundred and twenty of the local boats fished in the north, averaging £60-£80 per boat. It is interesting to note their expenses for the two months or so of the summer fishing, which were approximately £30-£40 per boat. David Watson (Pip) in the *Providence* was King of the Fishers with £350.

This year saw the greatest exodus so far from the East Fife ports for Yarmouth and Lowestoft; one hundred and fifty boats from St Monans and Cellardyke, and two from Pittenweem. In October, Skipper James Murray of Cellardyke, died. He was the pioneer of the Yarmouth fishing, as he first went

The *Wilson Line,* KY 322, the last steam drifter to be built in Scotland, 1932. She was slightly bigger than the standard steam drifters. After the Second World War she was sold to the Yarmouth Lowestoft area and was converted to diesel. She was reported to be operating in the eastern Mediterranean area in 1983.

south about 30 years previously. The best local boat in the south earned £200, and the lowest £6, the average being £35, and as the expenses usually exceeded £40 per boat, this could not be considered a successful venture.

1889

Again a disastrous year for prices. By the middle of January, English markets were overstocked with Norwegian herrings, and by the end of the month, prices in Fife had fallen to 6s.-7s. per cran. On February 6th, one hundred and forty-five boats landed 1,000 crans, prices 6s.-8s. per cran. The poor prices drove many of the bigger boats away to the great line fishing and with fewer boats going, the catches fell and the prices rose a little, but on the day of the season's best catch they fell again.

On February 10th, one hundred and ten boats totalled 1,200 crans, the price being 6s. per cran. But there was no day in March when one hundred boats landed a catch. The total for the District was one hundred and sixty-nine boats, 19,000 crans, 15,000 crans for Anstruther, average price 10s. 6d. per cran. In April, the new North Carr Light Vessel was launched at Dundee, a wooden vessel, 104 ft. long to take the place of the Trinity House yacht anchored at the North Carr. The great lines produced a fair remuneration this year as it had been prosecuted for a longer period by many of the boats, and cod alone was valued at £13,863 exceeding the value of the winter herring at £10,397.

On August 2nd, one yawl had 16 crans off the Billowness but this did not continue, and only 2,000 crans were landed locally for the summer. August 16th saw a new boat of 60 ft. launched by Jarvis for David Watson, the *Morning Star*. There was a slight improvement in the Summer Drave in the north and the local boats had £100-£300 per boat. This year saw one hundred and forty local boats go south, thirty-seven of them from St Monans. On November 1st, the following KY boats had 4-5 lasts each: KY 1822, *Maggie Brown;* KY 216, *Children's Friend* (St Monans); KY 346, *Hawarden Castle;* KY 159, *May Flower;* KY 2024, *Memoria;* £7-£9 per last (10 crans). The local boats totalled from £50 to £200 for the season.

1890

In January haddocks valued at over £1,500 were landed, but not much herring, and on January 23rd, ninety-four boats landed 150 crans at 35s.-48s. per cran. By mid-February, herring from Norway and Sweden floored the prices, and on February 11th, seventy-eight boats landed 500 crans, prices 7s.-8s. 6d. By the end of that week there were no offers at all, and no landings for a whole week as the boats lay ashore. By the end of February, several of the boats started the deep sea lines. The last reasonable day of the season was March 4th when sixty-five boats landed 280 crans at 10s.-14s. 6d. Storms and bad prices really finished the winter herring and drove the fishermen to the great line fishing earlier than usual. Whether this contributed to the disasters which followed is uncertain, but the depression which now existed in the fishing industry was to have new developments with the introduction of steam. It had been a poor winter herring, the District producing 6,000 crans from one hundred and forty-three boats, Anstruther 5,000 crans.

The first disaster was to be talked about as long as any of the locals who were alive at the time still remained to recall it. On April 8th the crew of the *Carmi II,* on their first trip, saw the Cellardyke boat *Garland,* fifty-five miles east of the May Island. They were the last to see skipper Adam Watson, aged 65, and his crew of 7 for the *Garland* foundered with the loss of all hands.

Before another fortnight was past, a Crail yawl was upset going into Crail harbour. Its two occupants, J. Brunton and W. Cargill were drowned. Brunton's body was recovered the next day covered with partans. (There is a similar story in Hay's novel *Gillespie.*) The paper said it was a very painful scene. (On the same day my father, with his father and Uncle Willie, had to lie and wait until the water made because of a high swell.)

Steam began to be talked about now in the District, due to the success of steam trawlers in Aberdeen, where the first locally built steam trawler the *North Star* (built 1883) had grossed £3,710 the previous year. That year, seventy-three steam and eight sailing trawlers regularly landed fish in Aberdeen and six new vessels were being built, valued at £2,500 each. This provoked local born Stephen Williamson M.P. to write a letter to the local paper suggesting the purchase of some steam trawlers in view of the prosperity of Aberdeen. By June, another letter from the House of Commons by Stephen Williamson said he had contracted to have a steam trawler built at Kinghorn, and he would retain any shares left after local consumption was satisfied. The trawler was to be 105 ft. by 20½ ft., and depth 11 ft. and made of steel. Before the end of June, J. Murray of Crail had a catch of 80 dozen crabs, a record up to that time. As for the Drave, from the District a fleet of four hundred fitted out. One hundred went to Shields, probably mainly Buckers, one hundred and twenty went to Fraserburgh and further north, and the rest to Aberdeen, leaving ten to twelve to fish in the Firth where the fishing was very poor, less than 600 crans being the total for the season. In the north, however, local District boats did better than for some years, averaging £150-£180, the best grossed £300 and the lowest £70.

Steam still dominated the topics in the letters in the local press and by the end of November there were three steam liners on loan, baiting their great lines with ink fish. No names of the liners were given, but the skippers were A. Keay, J. Birrell and W. Watson. These liners were said to be fishing well, grossing £60-£70 a week.

As for the Yarmouth fishing, it was better than average but with an unfortunate loss of gear. The average for the local boats was £150 per boat.

1891

This was a poor year, crippled at the start by a railway strike, which prevented many English buyers from coming north. Norway dumped herring into England and prices slumped so low that many of the men gave up. Only 6,000 crans were landed in Anstruther and 7,900 in the District.

There was a census this year and all the local burghs had a decrease in population, except Elie, which had nearly doubled its population since 1881. Kilrenny, including Cellardyke, decreased from 3,198 to 2,889; St Monans from 2,054 to 1,998; Anstruther from 2,000 to 1,700; Pittenweem from 2,119 to 1,991. On July 17th, Stephen Williamson's trawler *Faith*, KY 443, was launched at Kinghorn. She was 100 ft. by 20 ft. by 11 ft. and made of steel. She left for her first trip on July 24th at the great lines and landed a £50 shot at Aberdeen.

A few crans were landed this summer, the herring being caught west of the May Island. Most of the summer herring landed in Anstruther from this time on were from boats coming home for the weekend. On August 29th, twenty-four boats averaged 27 crans at 16s.-22s. from west of the May Island. (My grandfather had 15 crans that day in Cripple Jackie's yawl *Reliance.*) October 3rd saw the launch in Anstruther of the steam liner *Maggie Lauder,* KY 449, built by Jarvis—she was 88 ft. in length.

No information about the Drave or Yarmouth is available.

1892

This was the poorest year in the 1890s, another reason for attention being given to the development of steam. The year started with some promise as large shoals were found from Burntisland to Aberdour selling at 2s. per 100. However, down at the mouth of the Firth, the fishing never developed. January 23rd saw thirty-six boats land 120 crans, price 9s. 6d.-10s. February 6th saw fifty-eight boats land 230 crans, 10s.-15s. per cran and the season's best day was February 17th when sixty-six boats landed 350 crans at 7s.-8s. per cran. Meanwhile the new liner *Maggie Lauder* landed great line fish from 80 miles east of the Bell Rock, and on March 4th she had her largest shot of £62.

The winter herring season saw only 4,000 crans in Anstruther and 5,000 in the District from one hundred and eleven boats. The new steam liner *Rob the Ranter,* KY 458, 94 ft. by 18 ft. by 9½ ft. and 33 H.P. was launched in Anstruther on April 29th, and the *Anster Fair,* KY 461, was launched on 24th August. A steam liner *Edith,* built at Leith in 1866 and 66 ft. long, was bought during the year and joined the steam liner fleet and given the number KY 460.

1893

This was the best winter herring fishing of the 1890s. January 12th saw the launch of another steam liner *William Tennant,* KY 472, again 89 ft. and the *Glenogil,* KY 493, also 89 ft., was launched on 7th December. (This one was to lie for some time at the head of the west pier in my youth and so I know more about her than the others. She had no rectangular hold like the ordinary steam drifters, just a small square hatch.)

The steam drifter *Faithlie* leaving Anstruther harbour for the fishing in 1935. Among the drifters in the harbour are *Spes Aurea,* KY 81, *North Esk,* BCK 66, *Norman Wilson,* KY 228, and *Mace,* KY 224. In the foreground is the *Gratitude,* LH 28.

Details of the steam liners dominated the fishing news in January e.g. January 6th —*Anster Fair* £37, *Maggie Lauder* £31, *Rob the Ranter* £28, *Edith* £17. January 7th saw a landing which exceeded any day of the previous year. Fifty boats landed 520 crans, 8s.-12s. per cran and on January 24th seventy-five boats landed 750 crans, 6s.-10s. per cran. February 9th saw 1,000 crans from sixty-eight boats, 5s-13s. (N.B. any price over 10s. per cran was regarded as satisfactory), but later in February the English markets were said to be glutted. February 17th and 18th saw landings of 900 and 800 crans, 5s.-9s. The fishing continued generally good and March 7th, the best day of the season saw 1,400 crans from ninety-two boats 10s.-12s. per cran. On the same day nine boats had 45 crans in St Monans. This year was certainly well fished as the equinoctial gales brought the fishing to a quick end, the last fortnight not producing as much as 1,000 crans. Anstruther had a total of 22,000 crans, 24,000 for the District, the best since 1887. By June 23rd, the great line fishing was closed and considered very successful. The great line steamers went to the Summer Drave and were allowed to tow three sailing boats behind them at 1s. per mile, up to 30 miles. A total of one hundred and fifty boats from Anstruther and Cellardyke went to the Drave, and they averaged £130. St Monans boats averaged £120. At Yarmouth and Lowestoft, Scots nets had smaller meshes, so caught smaller herring and got lower prices, and it was regarded as a very poor Yarmouth fishing, average £80 per boat.

1894

The best fishings in January were up the Firth and no great catches were landed in Anstruther until January 26th when seventy-five boats landed 750 crans, at 10s.-10s. 6d. per cran. There were now nine steam liners fishing from Anstruther, some on hire. February saw an improvement in the fishing but prices were poor. February 20th was the best day of the season, when fifty-eight boats landed 870 crans, prices 3s. 6d.-6s. per cran. These low prices caused some of the boats to give up, as some of the herring fishermen were earning an average of 10s. per week, while the crew members of the steam liners had averaged £4 per week since the New Year.

The maximum number of boats was ninety-nine, the total for the District was 10,997 crans and 7,000 for Anstruther. April 3rd saw the launch of a sailing boat *Reliance,* 60 ft. by 19½ ft. by 9 ft. 8 in., for Adam Reid who installed in his boat the first steam capstan in Anstruther, a development which was to see the sail boat compete with the up and coming steam drifters at the herring fishing if not at the great lines, as they had not the same expense. This year saw an improvement in the north fishing where the above mentioned Adam Reid was King of the Fishers, grossing £400.

1895

This year saw the launch of another three steam liners locally, the *St Adrian,* KY 544, in Pittenweem and two in Anstruther, the *Copley,* KY 536, and the *East Neuk,* KY 546. The liner fleet was augmented by the Shields liner *Bernicia,* on loan to a Cellardyke crew.

No great catches were made at the winter herring fishing in January and there was only one good day's fishing in February. On February 19th, sixty boats landed 1,200 crans at prices of 3s.-12s. per cran. This was followed by a cold spell with complaints of northerly winds preventing the sailing boats from returning to Anstruther with their catches, the bulk of the herring having been caught on the south side of the Firth. After the large catch on February 19th, there was not as much herring caught in total for the rest of the season.

The *Spes Aurea,* KY 81, taking a big sea at Great Yarmouth. George Muir was in this steam drifter in 1938 when he wrote his diary, extracts from which are reproduced in Appendix IV. His father, John Muir, was skipper.

Only 6,800 crans were caught from a maximum of ninety boats for the District, and 5,000 for Anstruther.

This was a poor year locally apart from the steam liners.

1896

The last leap year for eight years was dominated locally by steam. Another four steam liners were launched for local crews. Three steam liners built of steel at Leith were *Kellie Castle* KY 567, *Isle of May,* KY 569, and *County of Fife,* KY 572, while the *White Cross,* KY 571, was launched at Anstruther.

In January lack of herring for bait forced the liners to bait with ink fish, caught by the trawlers of Leith and Granton. By January 31st anchored nets were being worked at Buckhaven and Largo. This had been a hard winter so far. Few herring and poor prices had sent most of the smaller yawls back to the small lines. One dozen Largo men were stationed at Burntisland digging lug for plaice for twelve yawls, as they were getting 10s.-13s. per box which compared favourably with the price of herring which had sunk as low as 1s. 6d. per cran. This year saw the smallest number of boats prosecuting the winter herring fishing since records were kept. Eighty-seven boats maximum, produced a total of 9,354 crans for the District, 7,000 for Anstruther.

Sailing boats were still being built and increasing in size as the steam capstan allowed them to hoist bigger sails. The sailing boat *Unity* was launched in St Monans for D. Corstorphine (Cellardyke). Another notable occurrence was the arrival of the telephone in East Fife.

1897

Seven steam liners all over 90 ft. long were built for local owners this year, with the *Fife Ness,* KY 589, being over 100 ft. She was built of steel in Aberdeen. The *Largo Bay,* KY 595, also of steel, was built in Dundee. Those built of wood in local yards were *Kilrenny,* KY 594, *Innergellie,* KY 604, *Rothesay Bay,* KY 611 (she was sold to Aberdeen as A 885 and came back later as KY 97), *Newark Castle,* KY 601, and *Curlew* (built in Dundee and numbered DE 91).

The winter herring fishing got off to its best start for years and on January 20th, sixty-one boats landed 970 crans in Anstruther, prices 13s.-22s. per cran. By the end of the month, ninety boats were fishing from Anstruther, including boats from Buckhaven, Newhaven, Broughty Ferry and St Andrews. By February 26th, however, the prices slumped once again due to the Norwegians dumping herring on the London market. On February 23rd, fifty-five boats landed 360 crans, prices 13s.-16s. per cran. After this, many of the boats gave up. It was nevertheless the best fishing since 1893, and one hundred and forty-six boats landed 12,000 crans for the District and 10,000 in Anstruther. April saw a lot of activity by the liners, sixteen steam and twenty sailing boats, which so overloaded the market at Anstruther that the steam liners started to land at other ports, mainly Aberdeen, Shields and Newhaven. June 4th saw sixteen steam liners average £36 and twenty boats averaged £8-£16 per shot. The best boat at the summer fishing was the *Lavinia,* skipper D. Birrell, with £540. On July 1st shortly before 7 p.m., fifty or sixty yards of wall collapsed at the west pier in Anstruther when the mud burst the wall with a loud bang which was heard all over the town.

In September, many local boats went to Scarborough. The year closed with the boats home from the south, with the best boat £400, and some discontent shown by the local fishermen against the liners. The steam liner *Largo Bay* was to go to Dundee as a trawler.

1898

Another poor winter herring fishing saw the steam liners making most of the news. Scarcity of herring coupled with the demand for bait by the liners undoubtedly helped to keep the prices reasonable, but the best day's fishing was on February 10th when sixty-five boats landed 330 crans at 13s.-17s. per cran. February 26th and March 3rd were the only two days which saw catches in excess of 300 crans. An indifferent season was finished off by a north-easterly gale in the last week of March. The liners had done well all winter and continued to do so. One hundred and one boats landed 6,000 crans for the District, 5,000 in Anstruther.

Steam was the word on all lips; even the Old Mill at the Milton Farm was taken over by steam. In September, Jarvis launched a sailing boat *Maggies,* 66 ft. long by 20½ ft. by 10¼ ft. (Notice again the influence of the steam engine, as the steam capstan was now used to hoist the sail.)

The greatest storm for 60 years, however, was about to hit the coast. The storm was at its worst on 17th and 18th October when Cellardyke pier was breached in several places, as was the gable wall of Anstruther Wester Harbour. At Pittenweem, the house on the rock was vacated and the pier at Largo was also damaged. A skeleton and remains of a stone coffin were found at the Billowness to the west of Johnny Doo's pulpit. Two stone coffins were also exposed by the storm below Ardross. Anstruther lifeboat could not be launched to answer a call for help and was dragged along the road to Leven by a relay of horses. But by the time it arrived the shipwrecked crew had been rescued by L.S.A. The year closed with the boats home from Yarmouth with a fishing worse than average.

1899

The year opened with most attention still on the liners. They had landed 16,000 cwt of fish valued at £8,900 in 1898 compared with 15,500 cwt valued at £7,500 the previous year. January saw only a very moderate start to the fishing, although the liners were much in the news—nineteen steam liners sometimes landing in Anstruther, but the first break in the ranks occurred when the steam liner *Copley* was sold to Shields for £1,950.

Best catch in February was on February 22nd when fifty-seven boats landed 800 crans, prices 7s.-10s. in Anstruther, but by that time the prices were depressed by eight cargoes of Norwegian herring arriving in Hull. Two steam liners were sold, *Glenogil* to Dundee and *East Neuk* to Aberdeen.

The 1st of March saw the best catch for the season, with 1,400 crans from sixty-four boats, but the prices fell to 2s.-6s. The prices really discouraged the fishermen and many gave up early, forcing the liners to catch their own bait. In the circumstances, the season was reasonable with a maximum number of ninety-one boats landing 20,163 crans for the season, 15,000 being landed in Anstruther. In the local District at this time there were twenty steam vessels and five hundred and forty-four other craft propelled by sails or oars, employing 2,200 men and boys. In May, at St Monans, Miller launched a sailing boat *Celtic* for J. Mackay (69 ft. by 21½ ft.).

In June, Fulton launched *Calceolaria* 68 ft. (said to have a steam winch). The summer fishing was the best for years. There was much concern over the decline of Buckhaven. In the sixties Buckhaven had over a hundred boats and now this had fallen to forty. The decline was blamed on men leaving the sea for the coal mines. At this time, Jarvis sold his boatbuilding yard to Miller of St Monans and a limited liability company was formed to erect a patent slip in Anstruther's outer harbour. The capital of £1,500 was raised in £1 shares. About this time the introduction of the bush rope made it possible for the steam drifters to fish for herring in rough weather. Twenty-five local boats engaged at Yarmouth and Scarborough averaged £500—said to be the best ever. The boats *Vanguard* and *Maggies* exceeded £900 each.

1900

Only seven steam liners prosecuted the line fishing in January which turned out to be a rather stormy month, yet the last day was to see good fishing as on January 31st, eighty-nine boats landed 1,000 crans in Anstruther, prices 40s.-48s. per cran. At the beginning of February, Fulton launched from Pittenweem a bauldie for Fisherrow and it was expected to become a type to be more extensively used.

The fishing continued to be good and 1,000 cran landings were made on three successive days from 6th to 8th February. Prices fell to 12s.-17s. per cran. the *Hawarden Castle* had 100 crans on 8th February, a very big shot for the winter herring. By the middle of February, there were 750 telegrams per day at Anstruther. There had arrived in Anstruther two Banff boats, several Berwick boats and a large number of Leith and Buckhaven bauldies. It should be noticed that this year marked the first mention of bauldies, presumably as the sailing boats had classified themselves as being the group of 60 ft.-70 ft. boats, whereas previously, in the 1880s and before, the boats had been anything above 40 ft. Good fishing continued until the last week of February when a

A view of Anstruther harbour, taken from the Chalmers Memorial Lighthouse about 1936, showing steam drifters berthed at the west pier.

south-easterly gale and blizzard put a stop to it. During this gale, a Shields liner the *Bernicia,* manned by a Cellardyke crew was lost with all hands. After the storm the fishing improved again, and on March 6th, one hundred and six boats landed 2,450 crans, prices 12s.-17s. per cran—the best of the season. That day ten fish trains left Anstruther. The final result was the best winter herring fishing up to that time. One hundred and sixty-five boats landed 38,916 crans for the District, 30,000 in Anstruther. During the year, the steam liners *Largo Bay, St Adrian, Kilrenny* and *Innergellie* were sold to Aberdeen.

In May, the new patent slip was opened in Anstruther—a 90 ft. cradle, 19 ft. wide on rails, 245 ft. in length. It was constructed by the boatbuilding firm of Miller and the engineer Balfour. The Chairman of the company was John Marr and the Secretary H. Watson. The first boat on the slip was the *Reform* belonging to Alex Rodger.

By now the steam liners had fallen into disfavour, as they were unable to compete with the steam trawlers in Aberdeen, and were too awkward to handle at the herring fishing, thereby making them of little use during the winter and autumn months. This created a boom in building sailing boats with steam capstans. In June, Fulton of Pittenweem claimed to have orders for six new boats. The summer fishing was said to be the poorest for some years with an average of £125 gross per boat. In September, Fulton launched the sailing boat *Cornucopia* for T. Bett of Cellardyke, and coastguard stations were provided with telephone cummunications. In October, there were three hundred and sixty Scots boats at Yarmouth and two hundred and fifty at Lowestoft. Well-known Fife boats were mentioned: *Paragon* 60 crans, *Vanguard* 180 crans at Lowestoft.

In preparation for the next winter herring, a rope was to be provided from the middle to the east pier to help sailing boats out in a southerly wind. In December, Fulton lauched the *Pride o' Fife* for John Watson (Salter) of Cellardyke.

The total value of fish landed locally was Anstruther £51,000, Pittenweem £3,500, St Monans £9,000, Crail and Kingsbarns £3,500.

1901

The ensuing year saw the steam liner fleet further depleted with the *Largo Bay* and *Fife Ness* sold to Aberdeen, the *Isle of May* to the Clyde and *Rob the Ranter* sold locally to be converted into a herring drifter.

By the middle of January, a Flanders frost (a south-easterly gale with frost, like 1947) with blizzard conditions lasting into February greatly hampered the fishing. By the middle of February, however, the fishing had so far improved that February 12th, 13th and 14th saw catches exceeding 1,000 crans each day, prices 20s.-30s. Mr Bonthron tried auctioning the herring without success. The following week saw continued success and February 21st saw a 2,000 cran day, followed two days later with one hundred and fifty boats landing 2,850 crans, prices 10s.-11s., while forty-six boats landed 474 crans at St Monans. What looked like being a record year, however, received a setback with a south-easterly gale in March and it fell away to a total of 39,197 crans for the District landed by a maximum number of two hundred and sixty-eight boats. Anstruther's total was 30,000 and St Monans 7,000 with the addendum that many St Monans boats landed in Anstruther.

An interesting local event occurred in March when the new Anstruther Post Office was opened on its present site. It was formerly in the High Street and it took over the building which had been the Victoria Hotel. This was an important move, as there were 900 telegrams arriving per day at the height of the fishing.

In May, Caddies Burn was filled up with earth from new houses being built in West Forth Street, an event which was beneficial to the carters. Another poor summer fishing in the north meant more boats fishing at home and 7,000 crans were landed in Anstruther.

The *Cosmea,* KY 21, later named the *Coriedalis,* which was the last Scottish steam drifter to fish at Great Yarmouth in 1956.

In November, an interesting piece of news appeared in the national press which affected some local men—a heavy fishing in Downing's Bay, Donegal. The Congested Districts Board boats alone earned as much as £6,000. By the end of November, the local boats were coming home from Yarmouth. The *Margaret Lawson* of Pittenweem arrived home after a passage of 36 hours. she was the best fished Pittenweem boat with £315. Fifty of the Anstruther boats averaged £150 per boat, the best being £400. It was the poorest Yarmouth fishing for year. The *Newark Castle,* the only St Monans steam liner, was sold to Shields.

1902

The year started with the sale of another steam liner, *Kelly Castle,* to London. Boats arrived from Newhaven, Prestonpans, Eyemouth, Peterhead etc. and a good fleet soon assembled. The best fishing in January was on the 28th, when one hundred and fifty-five boats landed 1,938 crans, prices 28s.-36s. per cran. Pittenweem was not often mentioned, but in the first week of February, Alex

Hughes's (Aitken) boat had over £180 gross for the week and 'parted' £20 12s. a deal. February 13th saw two hundred and forty-five boats land a total of 3,425 crans at 15s.-16s. 6d. per cran following two days when the total exceeded 2,000 crans each day. The next week saw four successive days with totals exceeding 1,000 crans per day. As the prices did not fall below 17s. per cran, this was good fishing which overwhelmed the railway, where sixty carts were waiting to unload at one time. All the smaller boats were well fished and produced the best quality. The biggest shots were got off Crail.

February 28th saw the launch of the sailing boat *Otway*, 68 ft. by 21 ft. by 9 ft. As often happened at the fishing, the catches fell away in March when extreme panic measures were taken. March came in with four extra telegraph clerks being sent from Edinburgh as 1,200 to 1,500 telegrams were being handled daily.

An interesting item about the fishing appeared in the *Dundee Evening Telegraph* — 'a sailing fishing boat with seven of a crew shared as follows: 2½ shares for the skipper and boat and 6 for the rest of the crew = 8½ shares'.

The greatest winter herring until the 1930s gradually faded out with only one day's catch exceeding 1,000 crans.

The end of March saw the demolition of the ruin which had once been Dreel Castle, the old home of 'Water Wullie', the fisherman laird of the Anstruthers. A maximum of three hundred and seventeen boats landed a total of 50,473 crans for the District and 36,000 for Anstruther.

At the end of the winter herring many of the local bauldies went through the Forth and Clyde canal en route for Donegal, under the auspices of the Congested District Board. (My father and his two brothers were in their own yawl *Expert* and were lying at Bowling when the Ibrox Park football disaster occurred. He was to have gone to the match with his oldest brother but was detained for some reason.) They returned in the first week of June but had fished poorly. On August 8th a local boat landed 111 crans in Anstruther from the White Spot. Four were towed in by a Dundee steam trawler. 6,000 crans were landed locally during the summer in Anstruther. The best local boat from the north fishing grossed £700. At the end of the Drave, another two steam liners, *William Tennant* and *Anster Fair,* were sold locally to be herring drifters. In September, a disaster occured when the Cellardyke boat *The Brothers* was lost with all hands—a crew of seven.

Thomson, the boatbuilder, completed a carvel yawl for Crail, said to be his 56th. He was a prolific builder of yawls (I was brought up in three of them). The end of the year saw one hundred and fifteen boats home from Yarmouth, average £350, the best being *Vanguard, Ina Cook, Breadwinner, Alices* and *Celerity.*

Anstruther harbour with the ring net boats from the Clyde. *Betty II* is nearest and alongside her are the *Morea*, BA 177, and *Aurora II*, BA 252. CN 264 is the *King Bird* of Campbeltown. In the background, the Folly is piled high with herring boxes.

1903

A boat later named *Elizabeth Keays* was bought by George Keay from Eyemouth. She was 70 ft. long. After the big fishing of the previous year, many of the stranger boats arrived rather early. By mid-January there were nine BK's, four LH's, four PD's, three FR's, three ME's, four INS's and one BF fishing from Anstruther. A large meeting of the fishermen decided against selling by auction. Not until February 3rd did a day's catch exceed 1,000 crans at 28s.–30s. per cran, and that from one hundred and fifty-two boats. Some of the Crail yawls fished well at this time, as the herring were off there. At this time, the Germans were buying the bulk of the herring and this maintained the prices. February 17th and 18th saw catches exceeding 2,000 crans per day and the prices kept above 22s. per cran. At the beginning of March in a south-easterly gale, one of the local boats broke her mast after leaving the harbour and was only saved when her anchor snagged on the telegraph cable which stretched from Anstruther Hynd to the May Island. The Anstruther lifeboat was unable to assist and the North Berwick one stood by. It was said that the Anstruther lifeboat could not sail to windward as she had no centre board and the local fishermen had lost faith in her.

The best day's fishing of the season was on February 27th, when one hundred and sixty-four boats landed 2,350 crans valued at 15s.-21s. per cran, one of the few days that year when the price dropped below £1 per cran. The season ended with a total of 32,676 crans from a maximum number of two hundred and eighty-five boats for the District, 23,000 in Anstruther. At the end of the winter herring, W. Sutherland was appointed chief cox and M. Gardner second cox of the lifeboat. Another steam liner, *Rothesay Bay,* departed for Aberdeen and Fulton launched the *Hughes* at Pittenweem for T. Hughes.

In May, a report came out with statistics proclaiming a record year for the Scottish fishing industry. Some of these are 'Boats propelled by oars or sail 10,722 valued at £944,814; Steam 375 valued at £1,391,445 (one hundred were not trawlers). On the east coast of Scotland, 1,358,270 crans valued at £1,360,492. One thousand and nine Scots boats landed 413,000 crans in England and 10,000 crans in Ireland (the latter valued at £12,546)'.

Two other sailing boats were launched at St Monans, *Star of Hope* 70 ft. and *Betsy Smith* 68½ ft. At the beginning of August, fifty-two boats landed 1,000 crans in Anstruther, prices 7s.-14s. per cran, and more women were employed at the 'farlans' by Bonthron on the Folly than had been seen for forty years. However, that was only a flash in the pan, as the summer landings locally were only 5,000 crans. The average of the local boats from the north was £240 per boat —said to be an average season. The beginning of October saw the sinking of the steam liner *Maggie Lauder,* the first to be built, in a collision in Loch Fyne.

The Yarmouth fishing proved to be below average for the local boats, but at the beginning of December there occurred an event of some consequence for the future of local fishing industry. The first steam steel herring drifter, (as distinct from the steam liner, which was larger) was built for East Fife. *Vanguard III* was launched at Smith Dock, Shields for M. Gardner & Sons. She was 82 ft. by 18 ft. 3 in. by 9 ft 1in.

1904

Cellardyke Fishermens' Union and Benefit Society had funds of £1,470, having paid out £68 for the sick and widows in the previous year. Their harbour, which had been given a complete repair from their own funds after the disaster when the east pier was washed down in the great storm of 1898, was now ready to be used again by the boats, who had had to use Anstruther harbour.

Fifty big boats and five bauldies prosecuted the winter herring fishing from

St Monans. The best day's landing in Anstruther in January was January 21st, when one hundred and forty boats landed 712 crans at 27s.-33s. per cran, while St Monans had forty-four boats landing 226 crans. February saw good average fishing with 1,000 crans being exceeded on at least five days, and 2,000 on February 16th and 17th. On the 16th, one hundred and sixty-five boats landed 2,645 crans, prices 14s.-17s. per cran. Trawlers at this time were poaching at weekends in the Traith and just east of May Island and the advent of the Fishery Cruiser *Brenda* was welcomed localy. The heaviest fishing was on the *Hirst* (off Crail).

The fishing in March was not so good and prices remained generally lower than the previous year, when the value fell from £32,000 to £25,000, but it was still regarded as a good fishing, as a maximum of two hundred and seventy-five boats landed 36,907 crans from the District, 26,000 for Anstruther. In this year, the *Elspeth Smith* was launched by Robertson at St Monans for James Smith and C. Marr & Sons had a new boat, built by Miller, called the *Ocean Foam*. In May, the Lifeboat Committee were given telephonic communications with the May Island.

Local Fishery Statistics stated that Anstruther had eleven steam vessels and there were 2,178 fishermen in the District. Anstruther and Cellardyke had one hundred and forty-two boats, 434 resident fishermen and 163 non-resident. Pittenweem had sixty-six boats, 227 resident fishermen and 87 non resident. St Monans had one hundred boats, 373 resident and 204 non-resident fishermen and Crail and Kingsbarns had forty-two boats and 78 fishermen.

In July, a tragedy occurred at Anstruther harbour on a beautiful summer day when James Deas's two sons were drowned, when one fell overboard and the other was lost trying to save him. (Their ages were twenty-two and fourteen.) At the end of July the new lifeboat arrived, the *James and Mary Walker,* 38 ft. by 9 ft. 4in., with 12 oars, double banked.

In August, great catches of mackerel were made off Kirkcaldy, the best for many years. The local summer fishing saw 6,000 crans landed, but the average from the north was the lowest for many years. There were five big boats from St Andrews at the North Drave; *Theodosia, Family's Pride, Fisher Lassie, Catherine Black* and *Nil Desperandum*. The average of Anstruther boats in the South was £180, Pittenweem £170.

The inside wall of Anstruther west pier was widened by concrete down to the cut mouth and part of it fell down exposing stones and debris belonging to the old pier originally built in 1753.

Meanwhile at Pittenweem, old properties dating back to 1620 were demolished at the shore. One of them had belonged to Captain Cook who

Steam drifters *Plough* and *Copious* stem on to Anstruther east pier.

carried Charles II over to Holland in his Pittenweem-built brig the *Surprise,* later renamed the *Royal Escape.*

The year went out with a decree which left its mark locally for the next half century and longer — 'All new boats must bear the registration letters ML'.

1905

This year saw more detailed reporting of the fishing. On January 4th, thirty-two boats landed 180 crans from between the May and the Bass. In January, James Muir of Cellardyke bought the steam liner *Innergellie,* and W. & J. Birrell bought the steam drifter *White Queen* from Aberdeen.

At the beginning of February, heavy landings of Norwegian herring in England brought prices down. February 23rd, 24th and 25th saw the fishing peak out locally with successive days exceeding 1,000 crans total, prices 12s-14s. per cran, with a St Monans boat *Isabellas* having 90 crans on the 25th.

On March 20th, a sailing boat of 70 ft. named the *Sunbeam* was launched at Pittenweem by Fulton for R. & D. Anderson of Cellardyke. She was to be the first successful motor boat for Cellardyke and the second or third of the District. A bad accident occurred with the sinking of a Cellardyke boat

Cornucopia by a Destroyer, resulting in a fatality when R. Smith was drowned. The Lieutenant in charge was dismissed from his ship and the crew of the *Cornucopia* received compensation.

Another successful winter herring fishing closed with maximum number of two hundred and fifty boats landing 39,273 crans for the District, valued at £31,898, and 25,000 crans for Anstruther.

A sailing boat launched this year was the *True Vine* built for St Monans owner David Marr by John Robertson of St Monans. Another sailing boat, the *Pioneer*, ML 30, owned by the Congested Districts Board, was fitted with a 25 H.P. Danish engine and attained a speed of four knots on her trial trip. She sailed to London, where the Secretary of State for Scotland and some Scottish M.P.s had a trip on the Thames in her. The cost of the engine was £300 and it did not prove a successful one.

The interest in the motor was now increasing, although a few more years had to elapse before the successful Gardner engine appeared. The average of the south fishing this year was £300 per boat.

1906

In view of the increased activity at the Post Office in preceding years, it was possible to obtain letters at the Post Office between 3.30–4.00 p.m. on Sunday afternoons. Many north country boats arrived by mid-January for the winter herring fishing.

A world-shaking event occurred in January when the French agreed to accept Greenwich Meridian. January saw below-average fishing and February opened with weather bad enough for the booms to remain on at Pittenweem harbour. (This was something that should be kept in mind, as for the next forty-five years the larger Pittenweem boats fished from Anstruther during the winter herring season.) The best fishings occurred on three successive days—February 13th, 14th and 15th, and on February 15th one hundred and thirty-seven boats landed 2,040 crans in Anstruther, prices 22s-23s. per cran. A steady fishing was maintained during the rest of February.

Fifty boats and bauldies fished well from St Monans, where the *Puritan* landed 50 cran shots for three successive days. March saw poor weather with poor catches, but the steam drifter *Vanguard* landed 30 crans from Dunbar Bay on a night of northerly wind when the sailing boats were afraid to venture near that coast where they knew the herring were. They got £100 for their shot.

34,303 crans were landed from two hundred and seventy boats, value £42,244, and there were 20,000 in Anstruther.

Two letters arrived in the District from San Francisco describing experiences in the great earthquakes (one said that there were thirty-seven different shocks). The locally crewed motor boat *Pioneer* had shots of 30 and 40 crans in Lerwick in June, and in July the steam drifter *Vanguard* rescued the crew of the St Monans boat *Puritan* which was wrecked at Lerwick.

Among many launches of fishing boats, were two steam drifters, the *Preston* at Pittenweem for G. Horsburgh and *St Ayles* by Miller at Anstruther for J. Stewart, the latter's dimensions being 84 ft. by 18½ ft. by 8½ ft.

August 8th saw the landing of 83 crans at £1 per cran in Anstruther by the *Nancy Hunnam* (my father was in the crew), when seven boats landed 420 crans. For the next fornight more boats landed at Anstruther than for many years previously and Bonthron's gutters operated on the Folly, and Melville's at the head of the east pier. (This I saw myself at some time in the 1920s.) August 14th saw 1,000 crans from twenty-seven boats, prices 10s.–25s. per cran, and on August 18th forty-two boats landed 1,200 crans. The *Topaz* had the best shot of 114 crans. St Monans also had landings of herring and on August 18th the *Elspeth Smith* had 48 crans.

11,000 crans were landed in the District for the summer season, the best since 1864, so it caused plenty of stir. It is not known if the catches were really local, as the boats had been towed in by steam trawlers. Anstruther claimed to have the best fished boats on the coast for the summer as the late local burst of catches boosted their summer earnings from further north. Steam drifters grossed from £600–£1,500 and sailing boats £200–£900. This was very welcome as it was followed by a poor Yarmouth fishing. One of the sailing boats only grossed £28 and one of the drifters £200, due mainly to bad weather.

One of the results of the good summer fishing was many orders for steam drifters, as many as sixteen or seventeen, and on December 7th Miller launched the steam drifter *Maggies* for A. & J. Gardner, dimensions 85 ft. by 18½ ft. by 8½ ft.

1907

The year opened with the biggest snow storm for many years, blocking the railway lines at St Monans and Stravithie. January saw the launching of the steam drifter *Camellia* by Miller at Anstruther for A. Aitken & Sons, St Monans. She was 85 ft. by 18½ ft. The fishing was poor during the whole of

The crew of the *Anster Belle*, KY 52, setting up their nets. They are J. Muir, R. McRuvie, W. Birrell, James Tarvit, L. Henderson, W. Muir, and R. Davidson.

January. Seventy boats fished from Anstruther and thirty from St Monans. February came in with reports of heavy landings at Newhaven from fishing grounds between Burntisland and Kirkcaldy; one boat having £160 for the week. From eighty to a hundred boats fished from Anstruther and thirty-seven boats and bauldies fished from St Monans, where it said the bauldies fished best. The number of steam drifters being launched steadily increased. March saw the steam drifter *Restless Wave* launched at Portgordon for R. & G. Hughes of Pittenweem, the steam drifter *Primrose* at Anstruther for Messrs Melville of Cellardyke, the steam drifter *Integrity*, 85 ft. by 18 ft., at Anstruther for George Anderson, the steam drifter *Morning Star* built at Portgordon for Star Jeems (James Watson) and the steam drifter *Unity* built at St Monans by Robertson for D. Corstorphine of Cellardyke.

The winter herring fishing was saved by good fishing at the beginning of March, and on March 1st one hundred and thirty-four boats landed 1,474 crans in Anstruther, prices 21s.-22s. 6d. per cran, and the fishing closed with two hundred and forty-five boats landing 29,630 crans for the District valued at £38,827, Anstruther having 16,000 crans.

The second week of April saw the arrival in Anstruther of a fishing boat whose equipment caused great interest and the effect of which is still seen today, although it took three years before it was imitated locally. The *Maggie Janes,* belonging to Swanton of Eyemouth, 65 ft. by 20 ft., appeared at the speed of 8 knots from Eyemouth, powered by a four cycle three cylinder engine with reversible propellor which could be feathered fore and aft so as not to be a drag when under sail. It was possible to start it after the lamp had been lit for 15 minutes. She carried sufficient paraffin for a 54 hour run, at a cost of 65s. for 300 miles. The engine was patented by Messrs McBain, engineers of Alnwick, and cost £700. It was also reported that six Eyemouth boats had ordered engines.

It is possible, however, that the *Pioneer's* experiences had an adverse effect on the locals, as it was decided by the Congested District Board to sell her as she was unable to compete with the steam drifters. May saw the launch of more steam drifters, *Venus* for Anstruther 85 ft. by 18 ft., *Tulip* at Pittenweem, *Magdalen* at Dundee for F. & M. Hughes of Pittenweem, *Evening Star* for R. Hughes of Cellardyke, *Alices* at Portgordon for the Betts of Cellardyke, *Azarael* at Sandhaven for Lawson of Pittenweem, *Pride o' Fife* at Portgordon for J. Watson (Salter) of Cellardyke and *Olive Leaf* at St Monans for W. Smith & others of Cellardyke. A good local summer fishing saw herring cured in Anstruther again. A total of 13,000 crans was landed for the District. Average earnings at the Summer Drave were £430 for the boats and £900 for the steam drifters. The Yarmouth fishing saw large catches with prices down to 2s. 6d. a cran. Boats grossed £14-£120, drifters £140-£800.

During the autumn, the steam drifter *Breadwinner* was launched for H. Bett of Cellardyke and the yawls *Thrive* and *Lass o' Fife* were built at Pittenweem. Among miscellaneous items were twenty-six naval vessels going to South Queensferry. They were seen from Anstruther between the May Island and the shore. Mr Burrows, photographer, received a letter from the Secretary of the King of the Belgians asking for a photo of a motor fishing lugger *Ibis III* (showing the general interest in power driven vessels). Anstruther Literary Society had a lecture from Frank T. Bullen who said his first skipper was Captain Smith of Cellardyke (whale's jaw bone). (This can be read in the *Log of a Sea Waif* by F.T. Bullen.) Seventy fishermen were attending navigation classes in Anstruther and Cellardyke, and Elie Ness was to get a lighthouse.

1908

January opened with a great storm. The St Monans boats, caught at sea, had to run for shelter to Burntisland and Granton. Three boats were destroyed in

Crail harbour, as they were caught without the booms on. Among the boats acquired locally were the steam drifter *Christina* for J. Mayes of St Monans, steam drifter *Clan Mackay* for the Mackay brothers of St Monans, the steam drifter *Calceolaria* for A. Horsburgh (Ogilvie), 86 ft. long and built at Pittenweem, while the steam drifter *Pursuit* was bought by T. Hughes of Pittenweem from Peterhead. The steam drifter *Lizzie Hutt* was launched by Miller at Anstruther for J. Hutt of St Monans and the steam drifter *Hiedra* at Portgordon for J. Smith. (My father's oldest brother 'Wull' was drowned from the sailing boat *Amethyst* on the 26th of February, aged 46.)

The winter herring fishing itself was the lowest since the turn of the century, the best day being February 20th, when one hundred and one boats landed in Anstruther with 820 crans, prices 21s.-25s. per cran. If the prices had held up it might not have been so bad, but they were actually the poorest prices that were to be recorded this century, when a maximum of two hundred and thirty boats landed 20,179 crans for the District, valued at only £15,993, 12,000 crans in Anstruther.

In April, the Congested Districts Board sold the motor boat *Pioneer* to Sumburgh, Lerwick. At the end of April, the steam drifter *Kilmany* was launched at Montrose for M. Gardner & Sons. She was 86 ft. by 18½ ft. by 9½ ft. In May, also at Montrose, the steam drifter *Carmi III* was launched for T. Anderson. June saw the steam drifter *Guerdon* launched at Aberdeen for A. Reid. These last three boats were all of steel and all for Cellardyke. The fishing in the north was only average, but many big catches were made at Great Yarmouth by the new fleet of steam drifters. Among them, the *Carmi III*—110 crans, *Lizzie Hutt*—150 crans, *Camellia*—129 crans, *Breadwinner*—100 crans, *Unity*—116 crans and *Rob the Ranter*—120 crans. Yet to compete with these, was the expanding fleet of motor boats in Eyemouth, where there were now half a dozen engined craft.

Locally, R. O. Jack, watchmaker of Pittenweem, became qualified to adjust compasses. Rev. Mr Paterson arrived in West Anstruther, a very important event for he became a great lecturer on navigation to the fishermen. In September, he announced from his pulpit that forms could be obtained from the Post Office for the first Old Age Pension and he would help anybody to fill them in. The year closed with the opening of the Murray Library in Anstruther.

1909

By the end of January, the Murray Library had over 250 members, and five guineas enabled one to become a Life Member. The first Saturday of the year saw the first Old Age Pensions paid and seventy people in the area received the sum of 5s. Eighty-two fishermen enlisted in the evening classes for navigation, and a motor boat *Jeanies* arrived in Anstruther from Cockenzie. She was fitted with an Alpha motor of 20 h.p.

Fishing remained very poor, even worse than the previous year. At the beginning of February, one of the six Eyemouth motor boats arrived in Anstruther. She was the *Britannia* with a 55 H.P. Gardner engine costing £550, but she still used her steam capstan. The *Maggie Janes* of Eyemouth had her capstan fitted to the motor, the first Eyemouth boat to do so. In February, Jarvis the boatbuilder died aged 74, and the sailing bauldie *Triumph*, ML 119, skipper J. Brunton, was wrecked up the back of Anstruther west pier, the crew being saved by crew member W. Wilson who swam ashore with a rope. The best day's fishing was on March 12th when seventy boats landed 496 crans in Anstruther at 16s.-18s. per cran, and so the poorest fishing for more than fifteen years ended with a maximum number of two hundred and twenty boats landing 8,000 crans for the District, valued at £8,000, only 3,000 crans for Anstruther. Most of the talk now was of motors for the big sailing boats and the merits of the various makes.

In April, a Portnockie motor boat the *Sardius,* powered by a 50 H.P. Thorneycroft, visited Anstruther. Another steam drifter was built at Shields, *Lily and Maggies* later renamed *Lena and Francis,* for J. Gardner of Cellardyke.

One of the best fished boats at the summer fishing was a BK boat that barked its nets with blue stone. She fished better than all the other sixty-odd BK boats. The fishing in the north was poor and so was Yarmouth where the local steam drifters averaged £400 each and the best sailing boat £200.

The problem facing the fishermen was whether the motor boat or the steam drifter was superior, as the day of the sailing boat was fading fast. St Monans opted mainly for the big motor boat and Anstruther for the steam drifter, with Pittenweem for both, yet mainly for the small motor boat.

1910

All skippers and second hands of steam drifters required certificates from the beginning of the year. Crail and St Andrews got new lifeboats this year, which were alas to be their last. The Crail one was *Edwin Kay* and the St Andrews one the *John and Sarah Hatsfield.* The average earnings of the seven Eyemouth motor boats at Yarmouth was £400, expenses £80, leaving £320 to be

A busy day at Anstruther west pier sometime between 1935 and 1939. The steam drifters are *Plough*, KY 232, *Breadwinner*, KY 253, *Acorn*, KY 194, *William Wilson*, KY 293, *Calliopsis*, KY 223, *Twinkling Star*, KY 347, and *Norman Wilson*, KY 228. The two drifters whose stems are nearest the camera are the *Pilot Star* and *Cassiopeia*.

divided into ten shares of which the boat got two. In Anstruther the first cox of the lifeboat was W. Sutherland, second cox M. Gardner, third cox D. Davidson. In February, the sailing boat *Majestic* of Pittenweem, skipper Andrew Anderson, was taken to Cockenzie to be fitted with a Gardner engine. This was the first East Fife fishing boat to be fitted with an engine which proved to be efficient. The fishing locally remained poor but it improved in March, the best day's fishing being on the 1st of March when seventy boats landed 720 crans, prices 15s.-17s. per cran. This was a year when the herring appeared to set inshore on both sides of the Firth. In the middle of March, stormy northerly winds prevented the sailing boats from getting near the shore in the Dunbar area, and the steam drifter *Vanguard* was taken off the beach, where she was laid up for the season, and fished strongly, close in off the Peffer Sands.

At the end of March, the herring set close in off Cellardyke and Crail, resulting in such good fishing that the Pittenweem yawl *Morning Star* sank off

Cellardyke with the weight of herrings and four of the crew were drowned. They were D. Muir and his son, and N. and T. Hughes. Only one man was saved. The yawls were hauled down off the beach and landed over 200 crans. This inshore fishing lasted until the middle of April. This helped the winter herring fishing to exceed the previous year's poor fishing, when a total of one hundred and eighty-five boats landed 11,364 crans for the District and 5,000 in Anstruther.

In April, a yawl equipped with a Grei engine was launched at Pittenweem by Fulton. She was named *Grei* and was 30 ft. long. The engine was 7 h.p. two cylinder, burning kerosene oil. The skipper was James Hughes (Wood) and she was the first of the 30-odd ft. motor yawls fishing from Pittenweem which could still be seen there fifty years later working mainly the small lines baited with mussels.

An amusing conundrum was propounded in Anstruther Sheriff Court in a case held at the end of the winter herring. 'How many tides around the May Island?' The answers were: 1st witness—'36', 2nd witness—'42', 3rd witness —'240'. The testimony accepted was 'No man can tell.'

At the end of May, the *Grei* was in the news as being useful in towing the big Pittenweem sail boats out of the harbour, as they set sail for the summer fishing in the north.

This was the best summer fishing locally since 1907, 14,000 crans being landed. Prices were poor, however, as most of the buyers were in the north. A summer of prevalent easterly winds saw sixty-six boats and thirty-two drifters fishing locally and large crowds of visitors lined the piers. The best fishing grounds were eighteen miles east of the May Island. At the Yarmouth fishing, the sailing boats of the District grossed from £50-£200 while the steam drifters had £200-£1,300, another year below the average.

1911

Motor boats now dominated the fishing news. In the first week of January, the Pittenweem motor boat *Majestic* was lying at anchor on the east side of the May, when two of the lighthouse men rowed out to see her engine. On trying to start it, one of the members of the crew, Robert Findlay, fractured his arm. However, Alex Smith who was present to see how the engine worked preparatory to installing one in his own boat the *Elspeth Smith* of St Monans, took over as engineer.

There was a big storm from the north-west at the beginning of the year resulting in a big loss of gear, mainly by the sailing boats, the value being estimated at £1,500. However, two of the steam drifters went out to look for the lost gear, and recovered about £1,000 worth. The fishing and prices remained poor during January and February and it was significant that the bauldies fished better than the boats, this also being the case after the war. The best day's fishing was on the 28th of February, when seventy-five boats landed 746 crans in Anstruther, prices 10s-11s. per cran, but the fishing closed early because of weak demand from the English market.

Although prices were poor between the wars, they were never generally as low as in this year when a maximum number of one hundred and eighty-six boats landed 15,515 crans for the District, valued at £12,463, with Anstruther having 7,000. In February the steam drifter *Golden Strand*, 81 ft. by 18 ft., was launched at Portgordon for Cellardyke. In May the steam drifter *Coreopsis*, 86 ft. by 18½ ft., was launched for P. Gardner of Cellardyke, She was of steel and reputed to be very fast. Those who admire John McGhie's paintings in the Fisheries Museum in Anstruther might be interested to know that he sold a painting in March for £175. At the end of the winter herring, three sailing boats of Cellardyke—*Sunbeam, Harvest Home* and *Jasper*—were fitted with engines by Parson and the St Monans boat *Elspeth Smith* came round to Anstruther to be fitted with a Gardner engine on the slip.

Eleven more Eyemouth boats were now fitted with engines, bringing the number of their motor boats up to thirty-five. The results of exams for skippers and mates resulted in twenty-three skipper's certificates and twenty-five mate's certificates for Cellardyke.

Details of the District fleet and fishermen were given as follows: forty-eight steam drifters, 1,067 resident and 385 non-resident fishermen, five hundred and nineteen fishing vessels of all kinds and two motor boats. Anstruther and Cellardyke had one hundred and twenty-one vessels, Pittenweem had eighty-five and St Monans had one hundred and eighteen.

During the summer, steam drifter *Andrina*, 86 ft. by 18½ ft., was launched at Aberdeen for T. Anderson of Pittenweem. The first destruction by fire of a motor boat took place in August when the *Vineyard*, not long fitted out with an engine, was completely destroyed in Anstruther harbour. Fortunately she was insured. There were heavy landings of lobsters in Crail in the late summer, said to be as many as 1,000 per week, a significant admission as lobster catchers do not tell things easily. The summer herring fishing had been quite good locally with the arrival of some steam drifters and motor boats and over 8,000 crans were landed locally. As there were plenty of steam drifters and motor boats now, no sailing boats went south to Yarmouth, although some fished from St Monans, where there was a slight improvement. Drifters averaged between £600–£700. St Monans sailing boats averaged £200–£300. There were now so many steam drifters wanting to lie up at the Folly at Anstruther for the winter that many of them had to go up to Alloa and South Queensferry. G. Mackay and his wife went up from Anstruther to Alloa to look after them. (I have talked to men at Alloa in recent years who remembered them living on board the steam drifters.)

1912

Fewer boats prosecuted the winter herring this year than in any year since 1900. There were several reasons for this, but the main one was the high running costs of the steam drifters. This resulted in several of them fishing on the west coast. The steam drifter *Dreel Castle* fished from Stranraer, *Rob the Ranter* at Stornoway, *Primrose* and *Capella* at Mallaig. The results of the census of the previous year showed the combined burghs which now made up Anstruther to have a population of 4,300, certainly in excess of anything after 1945. The winter herring locally started late because of rough weather. By the middle of February, eleven motor boats were fishing from Anstruther. The Cellardyke motor boats *Jasper* and *Sunbeam* had 11 and 15 crans respectively. The Pittenweem motor boat *Majestic* had shots of 20 and 26 crans.

February's best day was the 9th when forty-seven boats landed 406 crans at 25s. per cran. By the end of February, the herring set close inshore off Crail, and the Crail yawls fished on Sunday landing a total of 40 crans from anchored nets. The fishing continued light and the best day's fishing in March was 670 crans from eighty-five boats. The drifters had to give up at the end of the month due to a coal strike which caused so severe a shortage that the local factories closed. The drifters were laid up and between twenty and thirty drifters were overhauled and repainted locally. Many of the householders ran short of coal and had recourse to digging for coal at the sea shore.

The close of the winter herring fishing saw a maximum of one hundred and seventy-one boats landing 16,761 crans for the District valued at £18,742, Anstruther's total being 8,000 crans. Anstruther's patent slip became bankrupt and was bought by Miller the boatbuilders.

When the coal strike ended in mid-April, the steam drifters went to Kirkcaldy for coal, where the prices were 14s. 6d.–21s. 6d. per ton, but the coal remained so scarce that the drifters decided to draw lots for it. One of the St

A winter herring scene at Pittenweem, with local boats *Volunteer, Launch Out,* and *Courageous II*. LH 165 was the *Robina Inglis* of Newhaven.

Monans bauldies sank on passage with others to be laid up at Inverkeithing for the summer. April saw the launch by Halls of Aberdeen for M. Gardner of Cellardyke of the steam drifter *Plough,* 86 ft. by 18½ ft. by 10 ft. She was later mentioned as having 107 crans at Lerwick.

An article discussing the relative merits of motor and steam reported that west coast men were putting motors into their skiffs. The Moray Firth and Yarmouth men preferred steam as they had further to go to their fishing grounds, but the preference in Fife was mainly for motors. Another Pittenweem yawl *Quiet Waters* was fitted with a 7 H.P. Grei engine while the Cellardyke motor boat *Sunbeam* discarded its Parsons engine for a Beardmore.

On August 16th, M. Gardner in the *Plough* landed 167 crans at 30s. per cran, which at that time was said to have been the highest catch ever landed in Anstruther, while the motor boat *Sunbeam* had 78 crans.

A total of 8,000 crans were landed in Anstruther during the summer, mainly in August, as the herring shoals moved southwards and spawned at the White Spot and Long Bank, enabling Anstruther to be used as a landing port as the steam drifters and motor boats towed the sailing boats out and in. Statistics given for the previous year said that there were four hundred and fifty-five sailing boats in the District (only exceeded by FR and BCK), 1,012 resident fishermen, 420 non-resident fishermen, five motor boats and fifty-eight steam drifters, also 93 coopers, 234 packers and gutters, 43 labourers, 14,811,600 square yards of drift nets, 710,368 yards of lines and 4,320 creels.

The St Monans men had the best results for the Summer Drave, but many of the Cellardyke steam drifters were working great lines, and the Cellardyke men did better at Great Yarmouth where the steam drifter was more successful.

There were mass demonstrations at Yarmouth against the trawl, as one hundred and fifty Grimsby trawlers had been landing trawled herring, using nets 36 meshes to the yard, while the drifters claimed that their nets were 29 meshes to the yard. As the year went out the main topic of conversation was the picturedrome which was to be opened in Anstruther Town Hall.

1913

An extract from the Fish Trades Year Book for 1913 compared the fishing of 1863 in the District with that of 1913. In 1863 there were six hundred boats in the District valued at £24,000 and in 1913 there were five hundred boats valued at £180,000. In 1863 Buckhaven had one hundred boats at the Drave, but in 1913 only six. In 1913 there were sixty steam drifters, mainly belonging to Cellardyke, and seven large motor boats. January was dominated by gales and at the end of the month only thirty boats were trying for herring. The motor boat *Majestic* had 15 crans at 40s.-44s. per cran. February was also poor, but at the beginning of March, the herring set close in off Crail and on two successive days 90 and 160 crans were landed at Crail from yawls and bauldies, giving a maximum total for the season of one hundred and ninety-four boats landing 8,926 crans for the District, valued at £12,251 but only 3,000 crans in Anstruther. In May, Miller the boatbuilder sold all his Anstruther property, bringing all boatbuilding in Anstruther to a halt, and only yawls or launches were built in Anstruther during the next fourteen years until Aitken built the bauldie *Orion* in 1927. In St Monans, Miller installed a 14 H.P. Kelvin into the *Spero Meliora* of 38 ft., owned by A. Irvine, giving her a speed of 6 m.p.h. This was the first Kelvin engine to be installed in a local boat although it had been on the market for ten years.

The fishing continued generally poor and many of the older sailing boats were laid up for lack of crews.

Locally, Alex Smith secured the contract to supply coal to the May Island which then had a three hole golf course. (I rememeber seeing a seven hole course there in the 1930s.)

In October, Walter Reekie of St Monans launched a 28 ft. yawl the *Bird* for J. Bowman of Pittenweem. After a poor summer fishing, where failing supplies kept prices up, the Yarmouth fishing closed with the local steam drifters averaging £800 gross, with much damage to gear.

1914

The last winter herring fishing before the Great War was to be the best one for seven years and it was not to be bettered for another seven years. The Hull trawlers made news as the fleet were all to be fitted with wireless, a thing which even the best equipped steam drifters did not have until the 1930s. The steam drifter *Dreel Castle* went away to fish on the West Coast with other large drifters and at the beginning of February she had a 50 cran shot in Oban. By the end of January, there were as many boats landing herring in St Monans as in Anstruther. St Monans had nine fishing bauldies from 36 ft. to 41 ft. with 15 H.P. Kelvin engines. The motor boat *Ruby* had 27 crans at 28s. one day and the steam drifter *Vanguard* had 30 crans at 22s. another day.

The fishing proved quite good in February with good catches from the bauldies at the anchor nets. The best day's fishing was on February 18th when eighty boats landed 912 crans in Anstruther at 18s.-20s. per cran. The sailing boat *Midlothian* and motor boat *Majestic* of Pittenweem each had 35 crans, while in St Monans the motor boat *Mary Duncan* had 45 crans, there being twenty-eight to thirty boats landing at St Monans. The fishing continued good for the next two weeks and on March 5th, seventy-four boats landed 1,100 crans in Anstruther at 7s.-10s. per cran. The sailing boats *Jessie Hughes, Family's Pride* and *Amethyst* had 120, 100 and 96 crans respectively. On the same day fifty boats landed 550 crans at St Monans and the fishing was said to be partial.

The fishing closed with a maximum number of one hundred and ninety-one boats for the District, landing 29,857 crans valued at £32,065, with 16,000 at Anstruther. Crail had a poor year as the herring had hardly ever been close to the land. In April, after the winter herring, the number of boats being fitted with engines was seven at St Monans, three at Pittenweem and one at Crail. Thirty-seven steam drifters were manned by Cellardyke crews and ten steam drifters and eleven motor boats were based at St Monans.

1913 was a record year for the Scottish fisheries and one hundred and nine steam drifters and one hundred and sixty-seven motor boats were added to the

Fish, laid out in scores, being sold on the pier at St Monans. The man in the centre with the white collar is the salesman. The great lines can be seen on the decks of the bauldies. If the herring catch was poor, it was used to bait the great lines which caught mainly cod.

fleet. In the East Fife District there were three hundred and seventy-three sailing boats, twenty-seven motor boats and sixty-four steam drifters. Local resident fishermen totalled 1,386 and non-resident 368.

In June the fishermen were informed that they were not covered by the Insurance Act as they were joint adventurers. In July a statement about trawled herring said that landings in England had increased by no less than 86% in the year. Locally, because of the European situation, coastguards were stationed on the May Island. A lot of herring were landed locally that summer. After War was declared, fishing was only allowed in daylight at first. One of the insurance companies declined to accept responsibility for the steam drifters, many of whom were about to be requisitioned.

Trawling operations in the North Sea were prohibited and in mid-September the Destroyer *Pathfinder* was blown up within sight of Fife Ness. Two explosions were seen and a cloud of steam, after which there was no sign of the vessel. Wreckage was washed ashore from Fife Ness to Pittenweem. (The wreck of the *Pathfinder* still obstructs seine net activity to this day.) One of the local drifters was engaged by the Admiralty as a tender at £40 per month and £2 a week per man. J. Gen was drowned at Yarmouth from an Eyemouth drifter at the end of October, but no other information was given about Scots boats fishing at Yarmouth. The year closed for the fishing industry with rumours about the winter herring fishing being restricted to the daylight hours. Local rules were made which discriminated in some areas e.g. the twenty-three Pittenweem yawls were prohibited from line fishing but there were no restrictions in St Andrews Bay. The Destroyer *Success* was wrecked off Kingsbarns, the crew of sixty-seven being saved by Crail and St Andrews lifeboats, for which rescue the Crail cox, A. Cunningham, received the Silver Medal of the R.N.L.I.

1915

The year opened with an announcement that permits had to be obtained for fishing. Line fishing was allowed within half a mile of the low water mark, but anchored nets were to be allowed only to the east of Crail and there was a line of restriction from Fife Ness to the May Island, allowing drift net fishing only to the east of that line.

At the end of January, A. Thomson the boatbuilder who had built so many of the Crail yawls in Anstruther, died at the age of sixty-six. February 11th saw the most valuable shot ever landed in Anstruther up to that date, 125 crans valued at £416 from the motor boat *Restless Ocean*. The motor boat *Majestic* had 35 crans at £3.10s. per cran on the same day. By the middle of February, there were three steam drifters, nine motor boats and three sailing boats fishing from Anstruther and the steam drifter *Edith* had 118 crans and *Restless Ocean* had 107 crans. Prices fell, however, to 12s. per cran. At the beginning of March the fishermen were given a warning as forty-three fishing boats were caught fishing to the west of the line of restriction in the Firth and several skippers were fined £3 each at Cupar for this offence. The highest number of fishing boats mentioned was twenty-eight in Anstruther but no total was given for the District. 7,324 crans were landed in the District valued at £12,620 and 3,000 crans were landed in Anstruther. In March, W. Reekie of St Monans launched a steam drifter *Rejoice* for A. Davidson. This had been ordered before the War started. During the summer, the Crail yawls received a good price for partans but there was no demand for lobsters. Many of their yawls had engines now and in the District the number of motor yawls doubled in the year. Although there is no official record of a summer fishing by the steam drifters and motor boats, some of them were certainly at Great Yarmouth in the autumn, where the steam drifter *East Neuk* had a 160 cran shot at 32s.-35s. per cran. The steam drifter *Edith* had a shot valued at £467. Five local steam drifters were there and fished well, averaging £1,500 each.

1916

Anchored net fishing was allowed up to Kirkcaldy, half a mile from the shore during daylight for yawls up to 35 ft. and draught not exceeding 8 ft. A number of words no longer in use are included in a report of a theft of six iron truss hoops, two iron choffers and two barrow lifters from a curing yard in East Green. In January, anchored net fishing was a failure, but some of the local drifters were fishing well at Stornoway. This year was to prove the poorest fishing since 1879, the best day's catch being on March 18th when twenty-eight boats landed a total of 50 crans, which fetched only 50s. per cran as there was a shortage of railway wagons. The total landings for the District were 2,261 crans valued at £11,461, the latter figure showing the huge jump in prices. No total is available for Anstruther.

During the winter months, some of the local drifters had fished well at Stornoway and Mallaig, where the *St Adrian* grossed £1,763, the *Alnwick Castle* £1,624, the *Edith* £537 and the *Rothesay Bay* £1,173.

Some of the local drifters were involved in the evacuation at Gallipoli, including the *Carmi III* of Cellardyke and the *Andrina* of Pittenweem. One of the local soldiers told on returning from Gallipoli that he visited the *Carmi* when he was evacuated and was treated to a meal of 'saut herrin' from home. The poor winter herring fishing caused the Crail fishermen to turn earlier to the creels and on one day in May they caught 157 barrels of partans. In the week ending 1st June, they had sent away 626 barrels and 56 bags of wulks. Also in June, St Monans claimed to have broken all their records at the great lines while some of their yawls were catching herring at the anchor nets.

At the end of July, a Pittenweem and a St Monans boat were sunk by a German submarine and the Pittenweem skipper Alex Watson was taken on board. Later he was put on board another British fishing boat and arrived home safely. A lot of herring were landed locally that summer and there were good fishings right down to the Northumberland coast, tempting the bigger boats into the region of the enemy submarines.

Summer Time which had begun for the first time on 21st May ended on 1st October and was hailed as a success. This year no Scots fishing boats were allowed to fish at Great Yarmouth and the year closed with fish so scarce that prices rocketed and the selling price of fishing boats trebled in a year.

1917

Very little detail is available on the fishing this year. However, the local inshore fleet was given permission to fish within one mile of the shore instead of the half mile of the previous year. Herring were so scarce in the first half of January that they were sold for 1s. 6d. per dozen. Thirty yawls and bauldies were fishing from St Monans but the January returns for 1916 and 1917 show that white fish was the chief factor in the landings and Pittenweem, which was the home of the small line fishermen, was the top port of the District.

January Returns for 1917			*January Returns for 1916*	
St Monans	£	930	£	285
Pittenweem		2,335		1,013
Anstruther		110		112
Crail & Kingsbarns		237		157

The best shots recorded in February in Anstruther were by the motor boat *Fisher Lassie* of Cellardyke which had 7 crans on February 15th and 13 crans on February 22nd at 51s.-53s. per cran. Most of the herring landed was from the anchor nets, and on February 22nd twenty-four boats landed 128 crans valued at £479.

Cod net fishing proved very successful in February and March, averaging from seven to eleven score of cod per boat, mainly sold at Pittenweem.

Boatbuilding was still going on and at Pittenweem, Fulton launched a bauldie, *Julie Wood* 40 ft., with a 30 H.P. Kelvin engine, for James Wood of St Monans.

The weather continued so stormy in March that prices rose to a new record high of 286s. per cran. Thirty boats kept fishing from Anstruther, but no maximum number of boats for the District was given and a total catch of 5,659 crans valued at £28,934 was landed in the District. Very little information is available for the rest of the year although at the beginning of October, six motor boats from St Monans and one from Anstruther were said to have left for the south, accompanied by the usual convoy.

1918

Even less information is available about the fishing this year, the last of the Great War. There was only one mention in March of the steam drifter *Daisy* having been overhauled on the slip and on March 14th, the top boat of the week grossed £220 as the prices soared from £8 10s.–£11 per cran. The herring must have been very scarce. A large cigar shaped airship flew over Anstruther.

In April the fishing revived when catches of 2 to 8 crans were landed at £15 per cran. In the District one hundred and forty boats landed a total of 1,975 crans valued at £17,877, the lowest total value since 1855 and the highest average price ever.

Local boats were at Great Yarmouth. (My father was struck down by the 'flu, epidemic there, and was brought home by train by my mother and uncle at their own risk on November 21st. The reason I remember the date is because I saw him arriving home as I stood at the window of 12 West Forth Street all day looking at ships. As the local paper reported 'Last Thursday forenoon in bright sunshine double lines of British ships, six miles apart, sailed up the Firth with the German fleet between them.' Some were anchored in Largo Bay, others near Inchkeith. It was the day of the surrender of the German fleet.)

1919

One of the differences from the 1939 War was that not all the steam drifters were taken for the services. The following fished throughout the 1914-18 War—*Rothesay Bay, White Queen, Innergellie, Rob the Ranter, Alnwick Castle, Edith* and *St Adrian*.

January proved a very poor month at the winter herring fishing, but the controlled price was £6 6s. per cran. One incident which I recall was seeing an aircraft being towed into Anstruther harbour. A Flight Cadet from Crail landed in the sea about a mile off Cellardyke harbour and the aircraft stayed afloat enabling the pilot to be rescued. Although the War was over, drift net fishing was still not allowed in the Firth, so the main landings were of white fish from cod nets and great lines. Hawking of herring through the towns recommenced at the price of 2d. per herring. The best shot in February was 63 crans by the *Never Can Tell* of Pittenweem at the control price of £6 6s. per cran. The fishing improved in March and the best shot reported was in St Monans where the *Livelihood* had 83 crans valued at £530. At no time during the season was the number of boats reported, but eighteen large boats and a number of

Two Fifies in St Monans harbour. At work on the *Harvest Moon* are D. Allan, J. Butters, D. Morris and J. Gowans. In the background is the *Paragon*, KY 54, the most consistent fisher at the winter herring between the Wars.

bauldies were fishing from St Monans. The catch for the District was 5,033 crans valued at £31,622, 2,000 crans being landed in Anstruther.

In May, the Treasury announced the sale at cost price of four hundred trawlers and drifters built during the War. On June 19th, Britain's largest airship passed over East Fife on its trial cruise before its flight to America. On July 19th, Peace Day was celebrated by bonfires on the hills That on Kellie Law was quite visible and some people claimed to have seen one on Arthur Seat in Edinburgh. On July 24th, the Cellardyke fishermen went on strike against the owners, one hundred and twenty-one of their number being members of the National Sailors and Fishermens Union. The local president was Robert Ritchie and the committee were P. Smith, J. Wood, D. Watson, James Wilson, G. Doig, M. McRuvie, W. Martin and W. Davidson. They wanted the 18th share principle, that is 6 shares to the boat, 6 shares to the nets and 6 shares to the crew, which was the method employed at Peterhead. The strike affected twenty-six drifters in Anstruther, but only two in St Monans.

Letters appeared in the local papers about the fishermen's strike, one of them from Eyemouth, which may have had considerable influence, as it said the Cellardyke owners were claiming 7% more than they were getting before the War, and on September 18th, the owners conceded the men's demands after a nine-week strike. The terms of the strike were:

1. 6 to boat, 6 to crew, 6 to nets. All working expenses deducted from gross.
2. Scummed herrings to be divided as usual.
3. Mackerel—£1 per man as stoker, otherwise included in gross.
4. Black squad—Engineer 16s. 10d. per day. Firemen 15s. 4d. per day. If steam required before 3 a.m. on Monday morning, firemen to be allowed 5s.
5. Crew to be paid 15s. per man for scrubbing and painting ships' bottom.

Now that more men were home from the services, some of the young fishermen had difficulty in getting berths and seventy Cellardyke men went to Yarmouth in St Monans boats. After another poor fishing in the south many of the boats changed hands.

1920

Several of the drifters left for Stornoway. January saw very poor fishing locally, only the cod nets producing good catches. Before the end of January, there arrived the representatives of Burgon and Beazor, two names that were to be in Anstruther as long as there was a winter herring fishing. At the beginning of February, the old age pension increased from 7s. 6d. to 10s. per week and so it remained until the 1939 War. January did not see gross catches exceeding 100 crans and typical catches were the *Lily* 7 baskets, the *Breadwinner* 6 baskets on February 12th. On February 21st, the *Corn Rig* had 26 crans at 98s. per cran. March 10th saw an improvement in the fishing, presumably from the drift nets, when 500 crans were landed in Anstruther. The catches were rather spotty and the *Coralia* had 120 crans, the *Auricula* had 80 crans, the *Breadwinner* had 70 crans, the *Lily* had 46 crans, the *Hughes* had 45 crans, with prices ranging from 40s.-55s. This was the only good week of the season, which closed with a maximum number of one hundred and two boats landing 4,162 crans valued at £12,561 for the District. On April 8th, the following drifters left for the great line fishing; *Vanguard, Kilmany, J.E.C.M.* and *Lasher,* the latter being the first standard steel drifter built during the War to be reported in the District. In June, the steam drifters *Evening Star* and *Morning Star* were launched from the patent slip, where they had lain in parallel for several months. Both were wooden drifters and were given practically new bottoms to replace planks which had been worm-eaten during the War. July saw enough herring landed in Anstruther to enable the gutters to operate on the Folly and at the head of the east pier for the first time since 1914. The fishing in the north was reported to be very poor and the local fleets were coming home at the weekends in July and August and landing catches of 30 and 40 cran shots. By the end of August, Peterhead and Fraserburgh reported the worst summer fishing for thirty years and when the government controlled price of 45s. per cran ceased at the end of August, prices collapsed. On August 24th, the steam drifter *Dreel Castle* arrived in Anstruther with 150 crans but only 50 crans were sold to the cadgers and she had to leave for another port. At the end of August, one of the principal fish merchants of the area, T. Melville of Cellardyke, died. He was also the principal buyer of crabs in Crail.

Yarmouth and Lowestoft received seven hundred and eighty steam drifters and two hundred and seventy motor boats from Scotland. Prices remained satisfactory enabling returns from £700–£3,000 by the local boats, the latter total being landed by the *Dreel Castle* of Cellardyke. But it was not without its toll as W. Gardner was drowned from the Cellardyke drifter *Venus*, and the motor boat *Paraclete* of Pittenweem was lost by fire fourteen miles off Great Yarmouth.

1921

This was to prove the most valuable winter herring fishing of the 1920s, the combination of a fair fishing and a reasonable price not being maintained in the following years. In the first week of January, some of the St Monans fleet who generally fished herring for bait for great lines were landing up to 7 cran shots at £5 11s. per cran, while four Anstruther drifters left that same week for the west coast. In the second week the steam drifter *Scot* had an 18 cran shot at £6 13s. per cran. The fishing continued good for the rest of January, the best shot being of 95 crans.

February, however, was disappointing with the best shot reported being 50 crans at 38s. per cran by the steam drifter *Pride o' Fife*. No running totals are available but it appears that the herring had come in close to the shore as the end of February saw good catches by the Crail yawls at the anchor nets. The best shots in March were by the motor boat *Breadwinner*, 33 crans at 37s. per cran, while the motor boat *Annie Mathers* had 20 crans at 35s. per cran.

The maximum number of boats for the District was one hundred and nine, who landed a total for the season of 24,907 crans valued at £48,740. A coal strike hit the steam drifters and a form of local rationing of ½ cwt. per household was run by the Council. When the drifters did manage to get to sea, they did well at the great line fishing and in May the steam drifter *Dreel Castle* had shots of £700 for 200 score in Shields, followed by a shot of £454. Twelve other local steam drifters were fishing well at Shields at this time. The coal strike lasted until well into the summer and coal was being dug down the seashore at Cellardyke and Roome Bay, Crail. A significant meeting was held in September before the boats departed for Yarmouth when it was agreed by a large majority to sell all winter herring by auction using the Bell to assemble the buyers. Apparently, it had not been done this century in Anstruther. Mr Addy's Bell was once again used, Mr Addy being one of the great fishbuyers who came here in 1849 from England. This Bell is now in the Anstruther Museum.

The north fishing was a failure and the south fishing was disastrous, with great loss of gear. The motor boat *Sunbeam* was home by mid-November, having lost all her gear. Of one hundred steam drifters and motor boats from the East Fife District, one-third were said to be in debt, the cost of the heavy loss of gear is shown by the fact that a new net cost £7. The best Cellardyke boat earned £800 and the best St Monans boat £560.

1922

This was one of the worst years' fishing in the District between the two Wars and very little information is available from men who were involved. The first week started off with some enthusiasm and St Monans reported more fish being landed than for some years, even shots as high as 9 crans, left over after baiting the great lines. After that, storms set in, mainly easterly, and the best shot reported in Anstruther was 18 crans at 26s. by the motor boat *Breadwinner*. In February, the steam drifter *Scot* had a shot of 25 crans at £2 9s. per cran. By the end of February, there was no longer any great incentive to take the boats to sea and at St Monans only six boats continued to fish. It was said that the high price of paraffin had put some boats into debt. Prevailing south-easterly winds in March were blamed for an early end to the winter herring fishing and the season closed with a maximum of ninety-three boats landing 4,327 crans for the District, valued at £11,536. The total for Anstruther was 4,000 crans. The end of April saw a major fire in Cellardyke when the oilskin factory of J. Martin & Co was gutted, damage of £15,000 being estimated. Only some of the new standard steam drifters had a favourable season at the

A busy day at Anstruther middle pier with boxes piled high along Shore Street.

great lines as the prices for the summer herring remained poor. Yarmouth also saw a disastrous fishing, the *Kilmany* with £600 and *Cromorna* with £400 gross being the best of the local fleet. 'What do you expect?' said one of the local fishermen, 'when the new Free Kirk minister went down the pier to see the fleet depart.'

1923

The winter had been so mild that raspberry bushes were bearing fruit in Cambo gardens, but the fishing was so poor that 'Stoker Day' was expected to die out in Pittenweem. The proceeds from the first landings of the year were usually divided among the crews equally, with no deductions for expenses, but owing to the depressed state of the fishing industry the custom was not observed in Pittenweem this year.

The fishing was so poor in January that the Pittenweem men continued to fish with their sma' lines. They usually shot their lines between 3 or 4 a.m. to land in Pittenweem by 10 a.m. for an 11 a.m. auction.

The Crail men had given up the anchor nets and put in their creels. The only good catch recorded in January was 32 crans by the *Linaria Alba* of St Monans, at £3 7s. per cran. Only two steam drifters were fishing from Anstruther and a 56 cran shot on February 14th in St Monans was the best catch reported for the season. The fishing staggered on to mid-April, however, mainly pursued by St Monans and Anstruther bauldies, who got good prices for herring bait for the great line drifters. The maximum number of boats fishing in the District was ninety-two, who landed a total of 7,808 crans valued at £9,357.

This was a poor year all round, as the great line drifters were hampered by a scarcity of herring bait. The summer herring fishing was so poor at Fraserburgh and Peterhead that many of the local fleet returned home early. St Monans had only fifty-three boats north, compared with one hundred and three in 1914 and they complained that it was one of the poorest on record. (My father, that year, was in the motor boat *Corn Rig* at Great Yarmouth and it was a poor fishing due to rough weather and poor prices. This boat was lost by fire in December of the same year.) The steam drifters *Coreopsis* and *Vanguard* were sold locally, a fact worthy of note in that they were smallish steel drifters compared with the standard steel drifters *Norman Wilson* and *Mace* which replaced them. In Pittenweem the motor yawl *Courageous* was launched, 32 ft. long with a 30 H.P. Kelvin engine, so the changes which had started at the end of the War were continuing.

1924

The year opened quietly. (My father was in the motor bauldie *Enterprise,* on loan to John Deas of Cellardyke, and on the second day of the year they anchored nets down off Kilminning Stone, where the Crail Aerodrome was later built, and caught six baskets. I remember it because I was present, standing on the fo'c'sle trap wrapped in my father's reefer jacket.) January had poor results as a rail strike caused many of the larger boats to remain in port.

The motor boat *Hawthorn,* skipper Alex Watson of Pittenweem, was destroyed by fire close to the May Island. The skipper's five sons were on board and one swam ashore with a rope, and a small boat from the Island rescued them. They lost eight coils of rope, sixteen great lines and three nets.

An interesting event happened at the beginning of February, when two St Monans bauldies *Vigilant,* T. Adam, and *Children's Friend,* J. Hutt, landed 'ringed' herrings in Anstruther, the herrings being caught up the Firth. The Cellardyke fishermen were so angry that they had a special meeting which decided that no more 'ringed' herring were to be landed in Anstruther. This remained so until the 1930s. Martin Gardner said that the destruction of immature fish must inevitably result in the ultimate destruction of the winter herring fishing.

February saw increased landings at all the local ports from St Monans to Crail with several days' catches exceeding 500 crans, with the prices never below £1 per cran. In the District one hundred and twenty-six boats landed 12,320 crans valued at £19,900.

In Anstruther, C. Ingram's kippering shed and adjacent premises were destroyed by fire, a site never built on again until the housing scheme 'Harbourlea' recently occupied that area. The steam drifters *Integrity* and *Suffolk County* were sold while the *Fife Ness* was added to the Anstruther fleet.

A sign of the times was an advert in the local paper intimating that crystal wireless sets were on sale from G. Nash of Crail, and that the opening of the Wembley Exhibition had been heard on the wireless in East Fife.

Some good shots of herring were landed in Anstruther and St Monans during August; the *St Ayles* had 60 crans, *Daisy* had 50 crans and the motor boat *Freedom* had 44 crans, all at 30s.-35s. per cran which were good prices at that time. At the end of August, the motor boat *Lily* had 40 crans and the steam drifter *Pride o' Fife* had 30 crans (something I never forgot as I saw the *Pride o' Fife* towing the motor boat *Lily* up from the White Spot, an area off Montrose, on a beautiful summer's day.) J. Watson was skipper of the *Pride o' Fife* and his son Salter was skipper of the *Lily*.

Seven hundred and nineteen boats fished at Yarmouth, the highest since the War where the East Fife boats in general fished well.

The year closed with a notice to mariners, which said that weather cones in future would be hoisted at the Anstruther Coastguard Station instead of the middle pier.

1925

As an example of the lack of attraction in the winter herring fishing to the new class of standard steam drifters, the steam drifters *Mace, Menat* and *Spes Melior* left in January for the west coast while the *Cosmea, Agnes Gardner* and *Anster Belle* started the deep sea great line fishing in the second week of February. Few details are available for January and the St Monans boats used the herring they caught to bait their great lines, as they were getting good prices for white fish at St Monans. In February 15 crans were landed at Crail at £4 the cran. The price shows the scarcity of herring and the location shows that the herring were inshore as the Crail men only worked the anchored nets.

Not until the middle of March was there a reasonable day's catch and on March 11th, 500 crans were landed in Anstruther, prices from 13s.-15s. per cran and 400 crans the next day at 12s. 6d.-14s. 6d. per cran. The maximum number of boats was ninety-one, which landed a total of 10,466 crans valued at £12,458. This was regarded as a failure and many of the smaller drifters had earned nothing for the first four months of the year. In Pittenweem, there had been little temptation to stop the haddock line fishing and by the end of the summer they were claiming to have had a good year, while the larger boats of the area experienced a lean year.

1926

This was the year of the General Strike, which happened in May and so did not affect the winter herring fishing. More details were given in the Fishery Office about the fishing during the first months of the year, than had appeared since the War. A copy of a letter which had been sent to Edinburgh said eighty motor boats and twenty steam drifters would be fishing from off Dysart to ten miles east of the May Island from the 4th of January to the end of March. What actually happened was slightly different.

The herring fishing was so poor in January that only one steam drifter fished from Anstruther and the small catches of herring were used for bait for the great lines. The salesmen's bell was rung for the first time this year in Anstruther on February 4th, when the motor boat *Fisher Lassie* landed 3 crans at £2 10s. per cran.

Until then more herring had been landed at St Monans. This was to have repercussions for Mr Aitken the fishsalesman used this fact to try to persuade the Fishery Officer to transfer to St Monans. However, this did not happen as the Fishery Officer's reply stated 'With the exception of the years affected by the Great War, this is the first year landings of herring at St Monans exceeded those at Anstruther.'

By the middle of February, there were more general landings both in Anstruther and St Monans, and in the week ending February 27th, a German trawler entered Anstruther harbour for a cargo of 'Klondyked' herring (iced and salted in large boxes).

March 17th saw the highest catch of the season when 400 crans were landed in Anstruther, prices 12s.-22s. per cran, the *Abdiel* having 85 crans. In the District, fifty small motor and sail boats prosecuted the small lines from Buckhaven to St Andrews. Most of these small boats continued the line fishing all winter and those who had tried the anchored nets early on gave up as most of the herring were caught south of Fife Ness.

The maximum number of boats engaged during the fishing was one hundred and forty-three, which landed 12,165 crans valued at £19,653. Some of the steam drifters had spent the first three months off the West Coast, and it seems likely that less than half of the 12,000 crans for the District were landed in Anstruther.

The general strike came in May, and there was an influx of motor conveyances by the fish merchants. Prices at Pittenweem were £1 to £2 per box for haddocks and 16s. to 25s. per box for codlings. Crail suffered most as they sent all their partans away and some yawls took their creels ashore.

When the T.U.C. called off the general strike, the coal strike continued for months afterwards and this affected the steam drifters for the rest of the year.

In May, shots by the steam drifters which would have made £300 at Shields were only making half that total locally. At this time forty-one of the local steam drifters were fishing from Shields and they had to get permits for coal. Ten of them got permits for 180 tons of coal at Methil and this started the habit of the drifters going up to Methil for coal rather than having it delivered to Anstruther by rail. This lasted right up to the 1939 War and many an Aberdeen trawler was wrecked on the Fife coasts during that time, en route for Methil or on the way back.

By June, coal rationing for the drifters appeared to be adequate, and since transport had settled down again, the steam drifters did better, the steam drifter *Cosmea* having a shot valued at £400.

August saw the last major summer landings of herring in Anstruther, but since the local Fishery Officer had been sent to Montrose for the summer, no official totals are available. However, the local newspaper reported that on August 24th, there were good catches landed in Anstruther; the steam drifter *Acorn* had 120 crans, *St Ayles* had 115 crans, *Bene Vertat* had 109 crans, *Venus* had 92 crans, *Carmi III* had 49 crans and *Violet* had 30 crans. Prices fell from £1 to 12s. per cran. Gutters were scarce, except for Bonthron's on the Folly and Melville's at the head of the east pier. (This was the last time I saw gutters at work in Anstruther.)

More landings were made into the middle of September. An article appeared in the local paper on September 30th about prospects of coal prices for Yarmouth. Dearer foreign coal was available in England and prices were expected to be anything from 55s.-£4 per ton. Because of the high prices for coal, Yarmouth proved an unprofitable season, the best steam drifter grossing £1,500. Over twenty steam drifters belonging to the Moray Firth came into Anstruther for coal on the way home.

A view of St Monans harbour showing Miller's boatbuilding shed in the background. The bauldie KY 171 is the *Celtic*.

1927

There were still over fifty steam drifters in the District at the beginning of the year. As January came in twenty-nine of the motor bauldies were fishing for herring on the Clyde, mainly at Rothesay. Eight of the larger St Monans motor boats were using the drift net locally to try to catch herring for bait for their great lines, but herring were so scarce that they had to get sea sheets from Newhaven and Granton, from the trawlers. Some anchored net herring were caught off Cellardyke. In the last week of January, the Pittenweem motor boat *True Love* had 13 crans in Anstruther, prices 41s.-44s. per cran.

In the last week of January, all Pittenweem and St Monans bauldies returned from the Clyde via the Forth and Clyde Canal. On February 6th, a Sunday, the Crail yawls anchored their nets and a total of 80 crans were landed in Crail, conveyed to Anstruther by lorry and sold there.

The fishing improved by the middle of February and on February 16th, the steam drifter *Breadwinner* had 35 crans. The St Monans motor boats landed good catches of white fish from the great lines. Catches continued to improve and on February 25th, 1,000 crans were exceeded, the first time since January 1921. This glutted the market and prices fell to 5s. per cran.

The local fleet of about one hundred was augmented by boats from the south side of the Firth and for the next fortnight several good catches were made. Prices ranged from 6s.-17s. per cran. Only in 1932 were prices as generally poor again. By the beginning of March, thirteen of the local steam drifters had given up the herring and were prosecuting the great lines east of the May Island. The fishing closed with a maximum number of one hundred and five boats landing a total of 14,942 crans, valued at £14,263, 7,000 crans in Anstruther.

Two significant launches were made locally this year. In January Walter Reekie launched at St Monans a Fifie bauldie *Jeanie Smith* for Arbroath and on May 30th, another Fifie bauldie *Orion* 49 ft. 9 in. by 15½ ft. by 5½ ft., was launched for A. Doig of Cellardyke, which had two 30 H.P. Kelvin paraffin engines. (This was a craft I was often aboard, in the harbour and at the anchored nets, as my father was one of her first crew members.) Many more of this general purpose type were built locally right up to the War. The overall cost of the *Orion* was £1,000 and it was the first built by Aitken in Anstruther.

Several catches of herring were landed in Anstruther during August and September, but never as much as the previous year.

By October 6th, all the local steam drifters had left for Yarmouth, including the six steam drifters who had prosecuted the great lines all spring and summer.

The Yarmouth fishing proved better than the previous year when expenses had been high, but the combination of higher prices for their catches and cheaper coal helped the steam drifters.

The year closed with the launching by W. Reekie at St Monans of another motor bauldie *Protect Me III,* 45 ft. long with two Kelvin engines, for R. Marr of St Monans.

1928

The pattern of fishing at the beginning of the year was the same as the previous one. The smaller motor boats, mainly from Pittenweem and St Monans, who were able to get through the Forth and the Clyde Canal, were pursuing the herring fishing from Rothesay, while several of the larger steam drifters set out for Stornoway or Mallaig via the Caledonian Canal. The middle of January was past before the first herring were landed in Anstruther. Good catches of cod were landed in St Monans from the motor boats but the winter herring fishing locally did not make much headway until mid-

February, when there was a week of daily landings averaging 280-300 crans. The best day's fishing was on February 28th when over 1,000 crans were landed in Anstruther, prices being 16s.-18s. 6d. per cran. Many of the larger steam drifters were now prosecuting the herring in the Firth and in rough weather they were landing their catches in Methil. The fishing closed with a maximum number of one hundred and twelve boats landing 26,505 crans valued at £28,585 for the District, 13,000 crans being landed in Anstruther. On August 2nd the second bauldie for a local skipper, the *Just Reward,* was launched by Aitken at Anstruther for D. Corstorphine of Cellardyke. She was 49 ft by 15 ft. with a 60 H.P. Kelvin engine. In the same week on August 4th, the motor boat *Ben Venuto* was launched at St Monans by W. Reekie for D. Smith of Arbroath. She was 49 ft. by 16 ft. with a 48 H.P. semi-diesel Gardner engine. Also in August, Miller of St Monans launched a 46 ft. by 14 ft. canoe sterned nobbie for Messrs Robertson and Short of Campbeltown, for whom he had built the first canoe sterned nobbie seven years previously.

In October, Reekie at St Monans launched the motor boat *Clan Mackay* 66 ft. long but only 18 ft. broad with a 72 H.P. semi-diesel Gardner engine. She was especially designed to go through the Forth and Clyde Canal. This was the first Fifie motor boat (as distinct from a bauldie) to be built in St Monans for twenty years and she was also the last of her type as comparably sized boats built later had cruiser sterns.

At Yarmouth only the larger steam drifters were successful. Bailie Carstairs had two bauldies launched at Anstruther. The first one on November 14th by Aitken was named *Winaway,* skipper John Gourlay, and the second on November 29th by Reekie, the *Onaway,* skipper John Watson. They were 53 ft. by 16 ft. with 48 H.P. semi-diesel Gardner engines. The first one was skippered by John Gourlay for about twenty years, but the *Onaway* was soon replaced by a larger boat.

The year closed with the smaller motor boats again fishing from Rothesay (from where my father sent a poem to the local paper about the Rothesay fleet). One pair of ring net boats had 1,100 baskets of herring in one night valued at £800; a portent of what was to follow in the Forth in the mid-thirties, although we were still ignorant of the catching power of the ring nets which was to help sweep our winter herring away.

1929

This year saw the launch of the steam drifter *William Wilson* at Aberdeen, the second one for the area since the War, the first one being *Refloresco* in 1924.

A St Monans boat unloading its catch.

January saw very poor fishing. In February easterly winds prevailed with enough snow to block the roads in East Fife. The best day at the winter herring was the 28th of February, when 800 crans were landed, prices being from 38s.-42s. per cran. On March 2nd, the St Monans motor boat *Promote* was run down by a German trawler while hauling her nets off Anstruther, the crew being rescued by the St Monans motor boat *Condor.* She went down in 16 fathoms with her nets aboard and mizzen sail set. (This incident is worthy of note as the local carpenters I have talked to are agreed that the motor boat *Promote* was the last boat on the slip way at Anstruther, but they could not agree as to whether it was 1928 or 1929, whichever was correct it was certainly not later than 1929.) The fishing went on this year until the middle of April, with the best catch reported on March 11th, when the motor boat the *Winaway* landed a 50 cran shot in Anstruther.

The maximum number of boats was one hundred and sixty-eight which landed 27,054 crans valued at £42,930. Very little information is available for the rest of the year, most of the interest being in the relative merits of different kinds of motor fishing boats. These were obviously about to take over from the steam drifters of which only six had been built in Scotland since the War. One steam drifter earned £980 gross, but after all deductions had been made the deck hands' share was £22. There is very little information about St Monans until the end of the year when the steam drifter *Kimberley,* skipper T. Adam, was the best local boat at Yarmouth with £500 gross.

1930

This was to prove an important year, perhaps only the advent of the Great War having greater impact on the local fishing. The first information of the major change that was coming is to be found in the records of the Fishery Office, where the January report said that there were two distinct areas of activity in the Forth, the vicinity of the Forth Bridge and around the May Island.

From Newhaven there were nine steam drifters and one hundred and seventy motor boats including seventy-two motor skiffs from the Clyde which caught herring between Grangemouth and Burntisland, getting good prices of 53s. 3d. per cran. In the Anstruther area eleven steam drifters and fifty motor boats were engaged in drift and anchor net fishing.

In February this latter fleet was augmented to forty steam drifters and one hundred and forty motor and sail boats, the latter being mentioned as there was a heavy fishing by the anchor net yawls between Pittenweem and Crail in the second half of the month. February 10th was the important date when two Campbeltown registered ring net boats—*Faustina* and *Mary Campbell*—attempted to land 8 crans of herring in St Monans. The St Monans fishermen immediately ordered them to leave and declared a boycott of ring net herring landings. The two vessels were welcomed in Pittenweem where their herring were sold at 70s. per cran. The last week of February saw landings in Anstruther exceeding 1,000 crans on several successive days, reducing the prices to 10s.-12s. per cran.

As Pittenweem put on the booms at their inner harbour entrance in rough weather the west coast ring netters could not land their catches there and a note in the local paper for February 27th reported that all the west coast boats had left for Newhaven and by March 13th the last of the west coast boats had gone home. It was at this time that we find the first mention of the nobbies. Thirty-five steam drifters were included in the fleet of one hundred and eighty-five boats which landed a total of 40,229 crans for the District valued at £53,978.

Some confusion exists about the role of the ring net boats in the Forth over the next few years. Angus Martin in his book *The Ring Net Fishermen* says that the west coast men did not return in 1931 and 1932, but since the maximum number of boats at the winter herring in East Fife was one hundred and seventy-three in 1931 and one hundred and fifty-three in 1932, one hundred and sixty in 1933 and two hundred and thirty-two in 1934, there were very few in 1933 and they certainly did not come back in numbers until 1934. However, the ring net fishermen from the LH ports of Cockenzie, Fisherrow and Newhaven, certainly landed in Anstruther during these years from 1930-1934. These included two well-known Newhaven boats the *Reliance,* skippered by R. Ramsay and the *Freedom* owned by the Wilsons. These were Fifie built boats and they fished so well that the skippers soon switched to nobbies, Ramsay the *Endeavour* and Wilson the *Gratitude.* They were known as the Baigies and fished well. The larger steam drifters now started to participate in the local winter herring fishing instead of going to Stornoway or Mallaig during the first three months of the year. (I am told the *Bene Vertat,* KY 20, was the first standard steam drifter to go to the winter herring and that was in 1929.) Prior to that, only the old wooden steam drifters and one or two iron ones like the *Scot, Carmi III* and *Kilmany* went.

During the summer, the local boat building yards in St Monans were busy building fishing boats and Reekie launched the *Kestrel* for Campbeltown. She was 52 ft. in length, the largest nobbie to be built so far. On June 24th a 28 ft. by 8 ft. nobbie-type yawl was launched by Aitken in Anstruther. She was named *United Burghs* to the order of George Mackay who was to be known until he retired as the skipper of the May Boat. She was a beautiful varnished nobbie and in her he sailed visitors to the May Island for many years until he retired after the War. He later had a larger vessel which he named the *Royal Burghs* and she was a service boat carrying fresh water and essential supplies to the May Island during the War. (He told me that in one year, he made 527 [five hundred and twenty-seven] trips to the May Island from Anstruther.) A very great seaman was George Mackay.

A notable event occurred on the 28th of August, when the grand cruiser of the German fleet scuttled at Scapa Flow. *The Hindenburg* was towed up the Firth to be broken up. She was one of many to make that journey.

The motor boat *Onaway* was sold in July and a new 75 ft. replacement was ordered to be built by Forbes at Sandhaven. This boat was christened *Gleanaway* 76 ft. by 18 ft. 9 in. by 8 ft., with a Fairbanks Morse crude oil engine of 140 H.P. She was expected to run at a cost of £8 10s. per week compared with £26 15s. for a steam drifter.

Another change at the end of the summer was announced by Johnston & Sons, Montrose, who closed their salmon fishing station in the Hynd at Anstruther. The summer herring fishing in the north was regarded as a poor one, but the Yarmouth fishing was a success. The motor boat *Gleanaway* came home to Anstruther from Yarmouth in 27 hours, the fastest steam drifter taking 29 hours.

Much talk was made locally about widening Anstruther west (potty) pier and M. Gardner, lifeboat cox and skipper, said it would be a waste of money but deepening of the harbour by several feet would be of greater benefit. (If you promenade down to Hanna Harvie lighthouse today, it would be difficult to disagree with him.) In December, the motor boat *Golden Chance* was launched for J. Bowman of Pittenweem by Aitken of Anstruther, and so finished a year of change, yet with some hope for the future for the rest of the thirties.

1931

St Monans started a movement against Sunday fishing. As usual they were the first boats to start the winter herring fishing using the first small catches as bait for great lines. January was cold and prospects for fishing so poor that the East Fife boats remained at Rothesay. The good fishing of the previous year had tempted the largest boats from other parts and M. Gardner Snr. was skipper of a Yarmouth steam drifter. Several of the local standard steel steam drifters started the winter herring for the first time and many crews bought new fleets of white nets. These included the steam drifters *Lasher* and *Cassiopeia,* the latter landing a shot of 100 crans on February 24th. (A' hauled between the May and the shore as one of the crew told me.) 1,400 crans were landed in Anstruther that day, prices from 18s.-16s. per cran. That same day a number of Newhaven ring net nobbies arrived in Pittenweem and that is the only mention of the ring net in 1931. The booms were later put on Pittenweem harbour mouth, because of bad weather, and as they were not welcome elsewhere this presumably drove them back to Newhaven. Only moderate catches prevailed for the rest of the season, which closed with a maximum number of one hundred and seventy-three boats landing 21,906 crans for the District valued at £42,354.

During January, a motor yawl *Eulogia,* 25 ft. long, was launched for Pittenweem by Reekie and the *Boy Alex,* 34 ft. by 12 ft., launched for Pittenweem by Aitken.

A view of Crail harbour. ML 369 was the *Sunbeam* owned by J. Watson.

Much publicity was given to the local motor boat *Gleanaway's* claim that out of a gross of £598 at Yarmouth the crew got £40 2s. 6d. a share (⅓ to the craft, ⅔ to the men and nets), whereas the crew of a steam drifter could only expect £22.

In April local bauldies tried seine net fishing between the Bell Rock and the May Island, where the Arbroath bauldies had been earning from £70–£90 per week. 'Pittenweem however views the seine net with disfavour and it is unlikely that any of the fishermen there will become converts to the seine net. They contend it will destroy their line fishing for haddocks.' So said the *East Fife Observer.*

Summer saw the poorest fishing in the north since 1925 and Peterhead claimed to have recorded its worst fishing for seventy years. The St Monans steam drifter *Casimir,* skipper John Smith, was sunk at Yarmouth after a collision. The south fishing was regarded as being a poor one, plenty of herring but no demand. The year closed with the launch of the first locally owned nobbie, for Aitken and Mackay of Pittenweem, the motor boat *Enterprise,* 36 ft. long with a 30 H.P. Kelvin engine and built by Reekie of St Monans.

1932

Fishery Office Statistics for the Anstruther District reported forty-three steam drifters out of a total of two hundred and twenty-two vessels, employing 1,021 men directly, St Monans having seven steam drifters and Pittenweem four. At the English fishing, the local contribution was forty-one steam drifters and twenty-six motor boats.

January was a poor month at the winter herring and depression weighed heavily over the fishing communities of the East of Scotland. There were 50,000 barrels of herring unsold at Yarmouth and Lowestoft, yet Russian exports valued at £3,000,000 of salmon were still coming into Britain annually. Norwegians were already dumping herring into Hull, due to the mild winter, and this contributed to the average price for the herring falling to half that of 1931. In the last week of January the last steam drifter to be built in Scotland, at Aberdeen, arrived in Anstruther. 95 ft. long she was also the largest and one of the most handsome of the fleet. The *Wilson Line*, KY 322, had David Watson for her first skipper.

February 16th saw the Anstruther steam drifter *Uberous* with a catch of 102 crans, and on February 23rd, 1,100 crans were landed in Anstruther with a 100 cran shot from the steam drifter *Venus*. The same day 550 crans were landed at St Monans where the motor boat *Brighter Dawn* had 140 crans and the motor boat *Elspeth Smith* had 100 crans, prices ranging from 17s.-21s. per cran. That same night, many boats got fouled up round the Carr lightship with a heavy loss of gear. (I still recall nets being landed on Anstruther east pier all mixed up and men trying to untangle their gear.)

On March 15th, 1,000 crans were landed in Anstruther, but prices fell badly to 6s.-10s. per cran and St Monans had a total of 850 crans on the same day. The next week saw a glut of cod in Pittenweem as the cod net yawls struck heavy shoals of cod, feeding on herring spawn. Some catches exceeded 20 score. The fishing closed with the last operations confined to the anchored nets, some catches being taken from the Auld Haikes, the area between Fife Ness and Kingsbarns.

A maximum number of one hundred and fifty-three boats landed a total of 27, 248 crans in the District valued at only £23,416, Anstruther having 17,000 crans—these were the poorest prices since 1911.

In June, stokers and engineers in the steam drifters won their unemployment insurance case, but the fishermen failed to get the dole as they were regarded as seasonal workers.

The Summer Drave was said to be more successful than the previous year, gross earnings being from £380-£770 for eleven weeks, but alas the Yarmouth fishing was worse than the previous year, the average steam drifter not exceeding £300. The year closed with power in the form of mains electricity arriving in the East Neuk.

1933

This year saw the completion of a £20,000 renovation scheme at Anstruther harbour, which included some deepening of the inner harbour and widening of the outer west pier (the potty pier of the masons of the 1870s). There was an official opening of the west pier on January 4th, in the presence of W. Adamson, Secretary of State for Scotland. Drifters had left earlier for the winter herring fishing this year as by January 11th the steam drifter *Menat* landed a small catch. On February 9th, ring net boats landed 140 crans, while the drift net boats were blank. The Arbroath boat *Floreat* had 65 crans while the Newhaven boats *Endeavour* and *Gratitude* had 35 crans, prices from 58s.-64s. per cran. It is notable that these were east coast boats and no west coast ring net boats were mentioned all year.

The best day's fishing was on March 21st when Anstruther's total was 1,450 crans at 11s. 6d.-15s. per cran. On the same day 500 crans were landed in St Monans and 280 crans in Pittenweem.

A maximum number of one hundred and sixty boats landed 31,230 crans valued at £36,766 for the District, 18,000 crans being landed in Anstruther.

The fact that there were only seven more boats added to the previous year's total of one hundred and fifty-three and that no west coast boats were mentioned in the local press, would give some reason to assume that the ring net had been pursued only by the Leith and Arbroath ring net fleet. In April, Reekie launched two nobbies for Messrs Robertson & Short of Campbeltown, *Kingsfisher* and *King Bird,* both 48 ft. long. In the same month, the new R.N.L.I. lifeboat *Nellie & Charlie* arrived. She was dedicated in July before an audience of 6,000.

October saw the launch of *Floreat II* for Arbroath by Reekie at Anstruther and November saw the bauldie fleet setting out for Rothesay, where the Anstruther motor boats *Orion* and *Winaway* were to try the ring net, not too successfuly as it turned out. They never tried it again. Yarmouth again was a failure, only nine of the nineteen St Monans boats clearing their expenses.

The *Endeavour,* ML 80, leaving St Monans harbour for the fishing grounds.

1934

There certainly was a large increase in the number of boats engaged in the winter herring fishing from the East Fife ports this year, and we can confidently assume that this was mainly due to the presence of a large fleet of ring net boats from the Clyde. If the Clyde nobbies had been present the previous year they must have been only in small numbers, but the maximum number of boats this year was two hundred and thirty-two compared with one hundred and sixty in 1933. Small catches were landed throughout January, both in Anstruther and St Monans, occasionally resulting in totals of up to 200 crans per day with good prices ranging from 57s.-80s. per cran.

An unfortunate accident happened in January and this was ultimately blamed for the 1902 record not being exceeded. The Granton trawler *Roseberry* went ashore between Crail and Fife Ness and the tug *Bullger* was sent down to try to tow her off. On trying to enter Anstruther Harbour at low tide she hit the rocks and herself became a total wreck. She sank right at the end of the east pier and was a hazard to the fishing fleet for the rest of the year.

In February, one of the local young men, Tom Anderson of Cellardyke, was lost at the fishing from the motor boat *Just Reward.* The fishing steadily improved and by the middle of February some west coast ring net boats arrived to fish from Pittenweem. In the last week of February the weather improved and several ring net bags were burst with the weight of the herring. The best day's fishing was February 20th when 1,300 crans were landed in Anstruther, prices ranging from 13s. 6d.-26s. per cran. The herring had set close inshore and a record of 100 crans were landed in Crail. The weather broke at the end of the month, keeping the ring net boats ashore, and this led to the best catches being landed by the steam drifters. *Lasher* had 100 crans, *Breadwinner* 75 crans, *Abdiel* 70 crans, *Venus* 50 crans, *Pilot Star* 50 crans—all steam drifters.

March 1st saw 2,000 crans in Anstruther and 950 in St Monans, prices 19s.-25s. per cran. Good fishing ensued during most of the month. March 7th 1,200 crans in Anstruther. March 14th 1,400 crans. March 15th 1,600 crans, prices 13s.-17s. 6d. per cran. March 20th 2,000 crans. March 21st 1,400 crans, prices 12s.-22s. 6d. per cran. Many nets were lost through the weight of the herring. Although the fishing carried on into April, Anstruther was sometimes closed, when stormy, because the wreck of the *Bullger* broke up and scattered debris across the harbour mouth.

It was certainly the best fishing since 1902. A maximum of two hundred and thirty-two boats landed 48,526 crans valued at £65,250 in the District. Anstruther having 27,000 crans.

Among local launches this year was the *Floreat III,* 52 ft., for Teviotdale of Arbroath, built by Reekie at St Monans. August proved a tragic month for East Fife fishermen. C. Anderson and R. Hodge of Cellardyke were drowned at Fraserburgh and W. Reekie and A. Reekie, both belonging to St Monans, were lost off Peterhead.

Prices were poor in the north and there was a glut at Yarmouth resulting in fishing being banned for three days. The price failure was blamed partly on Hitler limiting the amount of foreign exchange available to buy herring, and so the year closed with another poor fishing at Yarmouth.

1935

By this year, St Monans had five steam drifters left, Pittenweem two and Anstruther twenty-six. The Anstruther and St Monans bauldies started drift net fishing with the entry of the New Year. A control committee was set up locally passing its own rules. No vessel to leave port if fishing stopped. No Monday morning sales. Two crans or less may be sold privately. All samples to be at the sale ring by 8.30 a.m. and balloted for order of sale. Any samples arriving after the ballot to be sold in rotation of arrival. Selling to commence not later than 8.45 a.m. January saw steady catches of herring, with no day's total landings exceeding 300 crans so prices remained up, usually above 40s. per cran. February 15th saw a total of 1,100 crans at 27s.-33s. per cran with a good fishing the next week when the 19th February saw about a hundred boats landing 1,800 crans, prices 20s.-25s. per cran. A lot of cod was landed in Pittenweem from the cod nets while St Monans best day was also 19th February with a total of 620 crans. February 26th saw a 1,200 crans total in Anstruther, prices 25s.-29s. 6d. per cran. Now followed the best week's fishing so far:- March 1st 1,300 crans, March 2nd 1,000 crans followed by a Sunday when no fishing was allowed. March 5th 2,150 crans, March 6th 2,200 crans. This brought down the prices, which had previously stood up well, to 17s.-22s. per cran. March 7th saw a 1,500 cran total, prices 13s.-18s. 6d. per cran. On these same days St Monans saw totals of 800, 500, 750, 550 and 400 crans respectively. March 8th saw 1,400 crans, March 9th 1,500 crans, March 12th 900 crans, March 13th 1,500 crans, March 14th 1,200 crans, prices ranging all week from 12s.-19s. per cran. St Monans had 700, 900, 300 and 450 crans on the same days.

These record breaking figures could not continue and March 20th and 22nd with 1,100 crans each day saw the climax to the fishing with prices of 18s.-24s. per cran.

The fishing staggered on until April 18th, and since this was much later than usual, different figures are recorded in Edinburgh's Fishery Board Offices, than were listed by John Lawson the Fishery Officer in Anstruther at that time. His figures, which include the catches up to 18th April, show that two hundred and seventy-five boats, seventy-seven steam drifters and one hundred and ninety-eight motor boats landed 58,322 crans for the District valued at £72,687, 34,000 in Anstruther, beating the previous record of 1902 when the total was 50,473 crans valued at £70,371 from three hundred and seventeen boats (mainly sail boats).

A notable event in the Fishing Industry happened on June 24th when the Herring Industry Board came into being.

The Drave fishing in the north was better than the previous year, but a disaster hit St Monans when two of their men, James Tarvit and W. Innes were lost overboard on their way home from the Yarmouth fishing.

When all was settled up after the Yarmouth fishing, it was found that the average fishing for the local boats was above the average for the rest of the Scots boats, and the local steam drifter *Twinkling Star* was the top Scots boat having grossed £2,100 and parted over £140 per man.

1936

The local winter herring fishing reached its climax this year. The greatest number of fishing boats caught the greatest number of herring ever caught at the East Fife winter herring fishing, although the total catch was exceeded in the Lammas Drave of 1860, and the total value was to be exceeded in 1942 due of course to higher wartime prices.

The start of the fishing was quiet and St Monans confirmed that the ring netters would not be allowed to land there. By this time they were landing in Anstruther and at weekends could be seen stretching nearly across the inner harbour from one pier to another.

What was described as a super bauldie, named the *Emulate,* was launched in Anstruther by Aitken in January for Messrs Aitken & Hughes. She was 56 ft. by 17 ft. with an 80 H.P. diesel engine. February saw a good steady fishing, but not until February 27th, did the total exceed 1,000 crans. That day, 1,210 crans were landed at Anstruther and 500 at St Monans, prices 31s.-38s. per cran. The fishing was general. The best drift net boats were *Lasher* 50 crans, *Adoration* (PD) 40 crans, *Transcend* (BCK) and *Evening Star* 35 crans each, *Violet* 33 crans, *Breadwinner* 32 crans and the best ring net boats *Virginia* (BA) 30 crans, *Margarita* (BA) 26 crans, *Veronica* (BA) 25 crans.

March 6th saw the start of the heavy landings. Anstruther's total was 2,320 crans at 22s.-27s. 6d. a cran. The best boats were:- Drift Net—*Betsy Slater* (BF) 145 crans, *Wilson Line* 100 crans, *Breadwinner* 100 crans, *Pilot Star* 90 crans, *Mace* 80 crans, *North Esk* (BCK) 80 crans, *Uberous* 70 crans, *William Wilson* 70 crans, *Rose Bay* (PD) 70 crans, *Heather Brae* (BF) and *Cassiopeia* 65 crans each and *Acorn* 55 crans.

St Monans total was 900 crans and the best boats were:- *Carmania* 85 crans, *Ebenezer* 80 crans, *Annie Mathers* 70 crans, *Diligent* 65 crans, *Emulate* 50 crans.

March 7th was Anstruther's record day for the winter herring with a total of 3,110 crans, prices 15s.-21s. 6d. per cran (Drift 1,300 crans, Ring 1,650 crans [Methil 160 crans].)

The best boats were:- Drift Net—*Adoration* (PD) 75 crans, *Heathervale* (BF) 75 crans, *Enzie* (BCK) 60 crans, *Calliopsis* 50 crans. Ring Net—*Harvester* (LH) 95 crans, *Ben More* (INS) 90 crans, *Chrysolite* (LH) 80 crans.

St Monans total was 500 crans, prices 15s.-17s. per cran. Best shots:- *Chrysoprase* 90 crans, *Spanish Castle* 60 crans.

Being Saturday, the railway was unable to cope with the landings and lorries ran direct to a German export ship at Methil.

On March 11th, Anstruther's total was 2,860 crans (Methil 110 crans), prices 15s. 6d.-21s. a cran. The best boats were:- Drift Net—*Prime* (BCK) 80 crans, *Crest* (PD) 65 crans, *Violet* 65 crans, *Acquire* (BF) 55 crans. Ring Net—*Incentive* (BA) 95 crans, *Thistle* (LH) 80 crans, *Floreat* (AH) 60 crans.

St Monans had a total of 1,300 crans (a record) from forty boats, prices 15s. 6d.-17s. 6d. per cran. The best boats were:- *Chrysoprase, Ann Cook, Celtic, Express* with 75 crans each, *Economy, Vigilant, Providence* with 50 crans each. *White Heather, Protect Me, Faithful, Elspeth Smith* 45 crans each and *Paragon* with 40 crans.

March 12th—The total at Anstruther was 1,930 crans, prices 18s.-22s. Mixed. The best boats were:- Drift Net—*Ugievale* (PD) 65 crans, *Sunny Bird* (PD) 55 crans, Ring Net—*May II* (BA) 75 crans, *Endeavour* (LH) 60 crans.

At St Monans the total was 260 crans, prices 20s. 6d-22s. The best boat was *Carmania* with 40 crans.

March 13th—the total at Anstruther was 1,620 crans (Methil 120) prices drift net 19s.-21s., ring net 20s.-23s. per cran. The best boats were:- Drift Net—*Radiant* (INS) 70 crans, *Acquire* (BF) 60 crans, *Violet* 55 crans, *Margaret Lawson* 50 crans, Ring Net—*Gratitude* (LH) 22 crans.

At St Monans the total was 900 crans, prices 19s.-21s. The best boats were:- *Ann Cook* 100 crans, *Annie Mathers, Pursuit, Protect Us* with 40 crans each.

March 14th—Anstruther's total was 1,240 crans (Methil 190), very mixed, prices 20s. 6d.-26s. The best boats were:- Drift Net—*Cavalier* (PD) 55 crans, *Lemnos* (BF) 50 crans, *Cassiopeia* 40 crans, Ring Net—*Silver Spray* (LH) 48 crans.

At St Monans the total was 950 crans, prices 19s.-20s. 6d. The best boats were *Endeavour* 70 crans, *Gowan* 50 crans, *Chrysoprase* 40 crans and *Pursuit* 40 crans.

March 17th—the total in Anstruther was 2,210 crans, prices 15s.-17s. 3d., mixed. The best boats were:- Drift Net—*Unity* (BF) 140 crans, *Cassiopeia* 80 crans, *Narinia* (INS) 75 crans, *Alpha* (BF) 60 crans, Ring Net—*Floreat* (AH) 60 crans, *May II* (BA), *Fisher Lassie* (LH), *Mary Sturgeon* (BA) 50 crans each.

At St Monans the total was 600 crans, prices 15s.-16s. 6d. The best boats were *Harvest Moon* 60 crans, *Paragon* 50 crans, *Chrysoprase* 50 crans, *Olive Branch* (PD) 50 crans, *Diligence* 40 crans.

March 18th—the total in Anstruther was 1,050 crans, prices—Drift Net 15s.-19s., Ring Net 30s.-33s. 6d. The best boats were:- Drift Net—*Spes Aurea* 50 crans, *Fountain* (BF) 45 crans, *Violet* 40 crans, *Spes Melior* 35 crans.

The St Monans total was 400 crans, prices 15s.-16s. The best boats were:- *Courage* (BCK) 33 crans and *Lively Hope* 25 crans.

March 19th—Anstruther's total was 1,110 crans, prices Drift Net 15s.-18s. 6d. Ring Net 15s.-29s. per cran. The best boats were:- Drift Net—*Acquire* (BF) 70 crans, *Barbara* (INS) 55 crans, *North Esk* (BCK) 45 crans. The port was then closed as the minimum price of 15s. was difficult to maintain. This was a Thursday and the spell was broken as Saturday's landings were light and several of the north boats went home. However, the season was not over yet and on March 24th Anstruther's total was 1,870 crans, prices 16s.-18s. 3d. The best boats were:- Drift Net—*Orion* 50 crans, *Enterprise* 50 crans, *Good Hope, Acorn, Plough* 40 crans each. Ring Net—*Harvester* (LH) and *Chrysolite* (LH) 65 crans each, *Aliped V* (BA) 60 crans.

At St Monans the total was 800 crans, prices 15s.-17s. The best boats were *Faithful* 70 crans and *Elspeth Smith* 50 crans.

The Pittenweem total was 300 crans and the best boats were:- *Fortunatus* 70 crans and *Eulogia* 60 crans.

March 25th—Anstruther's total was 720 crans all by drift net, prices 15s. 6d.-19s. 6d. The best boats were:- *Cassiopeia* 120 crans, *Violet* 75 crans, *Calliopsis* 60 crans and *North Esk* (BCK) 50 crans.

The St Monans total was 300 crans, prices 15s.-17s. The best boats were *Ruby* 90 crans and *Lucy Mackay* 70 crans.

March 26th—Anstruther's total was 750 crans, prices 16s.-18s. The best boats were:- *Pilot Star* 65 crans, *Spes Melior* 60 crans, *Mace* and *Copious* 50 crans each. 1,000 crans in Anstruther was still to be exceeded on another two days before the end of the season.

March 31st—Anstruther's total was 1,290 crans. Drift Net 360 crans, Ring Net 930 crans, prices 15s.-22s. 6d., mixed. The best boats were:- Drift Net—*Emulate* 40 crans, *Lucy Mackay* 35 crans. Ring Net—*Aliped V* (BA) 100 crans, *Incentive* (BA) 95 crans *AJJ & T* (BA) 90 crans.

St Monans had a total of 700 crans, prices 15s.16s. The best boats were *Condor* and *Paragon* each with 45 crans, *Brighter Hope* and *Carmania* each 40 crans.

The Pittenweem total was 400 crans. The best boats were *Launch Out* 40 crans, *Fortunatus* 40 crans, *Volunteer, United* and *Trusty* 30 crans each.

April 1st—Anstruther's total was 1,440 crans, prices 15s.-22s. 6d., mixed. The best boats were:- Drift Net—*Orion* and *Refuge* 25 crans each. Ring Net—*Aliped V* (BA) 120 crans. *Incentive* (BA) 90 crans, *Morea* (BA) 85 crans, *Lily of the Valley* (LH) 50 crans.

The St Monans total was 400 crans. The best boats were *Paragon* 45 crans, *Lively Hope* 35 crans.

On April 11th, the *Amber Queen* had 114 crans in Pittenweem and the fishing had again lasted until the middle of April.

The steam drifter *Pilot Star* unloading its catch at the extreme end of Anstruther east pier, an unusual occurrence, showing that the weather was very calm. The skipper, D. Smith, is at the capstan and on the pier are A. Smith, J. Carstairs and D. Parker.

The maximum number of boats was three hundred and twenty-three; ninety five steam drifters, one hundred and sixteen motor drifters and one hundred and twelve ring net boats. The total for the District was 75,836 crans valued at £96,181. Anstruther's total alone was nearly 46,000 crans.

During February a disaster affected the community when the Leith trawler *May Island* was wrecked near the Island of Unst with the loss of all hands. The local men lost were the skipper James Tarvit, his brother John, D. Birrell, all of Cellardyke and D. Young of St Monans.

The local motor boat *Gleanaway* was sold to South Africa and her builder Forbes arrived to build a replacement on the bulwark at Cellardyke harbour.

At the end of May, Reekie launched a big nobbie the *Argosy,* for A. Lawson of Pittenweem. She was 53 ft. long and had an 80 H.P. diesel engine.

In July, the replacement for the *Gleanaway*—the *Royal Sovereign*—was launched at Cellardyke harbour, attracting a large crowd as she was launched broadside on. Provost Carstairs who had commissioned her said that her expenses would be only one third of that of a steam drifter. He gave the example of the *Gleanaway* grossing £438 and sharing £32 5s. per man, while a steam drifter grossing £445 shared £16 per man. The new boat was 69 ft. by 18 ft. 3 in. by 8 ft.

From the same berth on September 30th, another boat was launched. She was the *Star o' Hope,* 54 ft. by 18 ft., with an H.P. Paxman Ricardo diesel engine, built for John Stewart of Cellardyke and his sons-in-law, T. Ovenstone and D. Corstorphine.

In September, the *Floral Queen* was launched by Reekie at Anstruther for the Watson brothers of Pittenweem. She was 47 ft. by 15½ ft. with a 63 H.P. diesel engine.

The Yarmouth fishing for the steam drifters was, on average, £100 per boat up on the previous year. The best drifter grossed £2,050 and the average was about £630. Rough weather prevented the St Monans motor boats from doing as well and the fishing was marred by the loss, with all hands, of the Peterhead motor boat *Olive Branch.* The year closed with the launch of the *Girl Christian,* 53 ft. long with an 88 H.P. Kelvin diesel engine, for T. Gerrard of St Monans. She was built by Reekie at St Monans.

1937

Two steam drifters the *Mace* and the *Acorn* were equipped with transmitting radio. In an article by Dr. Henry Wood on the herring, there appeared a statement which partly explains the disappearance of the herring shoals 'of all marketable fish, only the herring, catfish, skate and ray have eggs which sink to the bottom'. This reinforced the fears of the fishermen that the ring net was responsible for the destruction of the spawning grounds. In mid-January, Anstruther's new sale ring was opened at a cost of £1,000. This was to be a very stormy year and this was the chief reason for a decline in landings. A minimum price of 15s. per cran was again decided by the local committee and for carrying out decisions on this, Anstruther and St Monans were to be regarded as one port.

Many of the January landings were by the steam drifters at Methil, showing that most of the fishing was done by the larger steam drifters. The first week of February saw the worst storm since the destruction of Cellardyke harbour in 1898.

More steam drifters than ever before from the Moray Firth arrived to take part in the drift net fishing. There were one hundred and thirteen before the season was finished, eighteen up on the previous year and the highest total ever. A well-known Pittenweem motor boat *Margaret Lawson* went ashore in fog at the Billowness and became a total wreck.

Pittenweem had the booms on their harbour so often that it was decided to petition for £8,000 for an improvement scheme and it was disclosed that booms had been used there since 1903. Not until February 23rd was there a good day's fishing and then a total of 1,140 crans were landed in Anstruther, prices 38s.-40s. per cran, with 300 crans in St Monans, where the *Condor* (ML) had 56 crans.

The second week in March saw an improvement which was ended by another storm. March 10th saw 1,290 crans in Anstruther, prices 38s.-41s. 6d. with St Monans 275 crans. March 16th saw the weather improve and this was reflected in the landings of 1,500 crans, of which the ring net boats landed 1,200 crans, prices 27s. 6d.-36s. 6d. The motor boat *Winaway* had 48 crans, but the ring net boat *Radiant* (INS) had 89 crans. St Monans had 500 crans that day, with the motor boat *Protect Me* landing 75 crans. Pittenweem had 150 crans with the motor boats *Launch Out* and *Volunteer* having 67 crans. The most recent storm was accompanied by heavy snow which closed all roads in East Fife but the trains managed to keep going. March 20th saw 1,280 crans landed in Anstruther of which the ring net supplied 680 crans, prices 32s. 6d.-36s. 6d. per cran. The best drift net boat was *Emulate* with 45 crans. the best ring net boat was the *Ardent* (INS) with 75 crans. St Monans had 600 crans that day, the best boat being the *Girl Christian* with 45 crans. Pittenweem had 300 crans with *Good Design* landing 70 crans. March 24th saw 2,250 crans in Anstruther of which the ring net boats landed 1,930 crans, prices 20s.-22s. The port was closed for the day as the market was slow. The best drift net boat was *Spes Aurea* with 49 crans and the best ring net boat *Lily of the Valley* (LH) with 100 crans. St Monans had 170 crans with the *Lucy Mackay* landing 68 crans. Pittenweem had 220 crans. The fishing continued well into April with only one other day, 30th March exceeding 1,000 crans, when 1,290 crans were landed in Anstruther. Ring net landing 850 crans, prices 25s.-28s. The best drift net boat was the *Pilot Star* with 30 crans and the best ring net boat was the *Lively Hope* (LH) with 70 crans. St Monans had 400 crans with the *Lively Hope* (ML) landing 40 crans. Pittenweem had 335 crans with the *Courageous II* top with 60 crans.

This was the first year that Pittenweem landings made a significant contributuion, due to their fleet adopting the ring net. The maximum number of boats was three hundred and thirteen (one hundred and thirteen steam drifters and two hundred motor boats) landing 36,080 crans valued at £65,947 for the District, Anstruther having 21,000 crans.

Two notable launches occurred in April. On April 14th the *Taeping,* 70 ft. long, was launched for Henry Bett of Cellardyke. She was built in Anstruther by Reekie and had a 96 H.P. semi-diesel engine. She was the third of this name, the skipper Henry Bett being the grandson of the first owner.

The *Gleanaway*, KY 40, the first local boat with a cruiser stern, setting off on her trial trip.

On 29th April, Aitken launched the *Vesper*, 60 ft. by 18 ft. for James Cargill of St Monans. She had a 105 H.P. Atlantic diesel engine.

In June, two nobbies were launched broadside on at Cellardyke harbour. They were the *Manx Beauty* and the *Manx Fairy* and were destined for Peel. In July, a Pilot Cutter was launched in the same place.

It had been decided to deepen Anstruther Inner Harbour and it was closed at the beginning of July for the erection of a Coffer Dam built by R. Terras. When this was completed work commenced on the deepening of the inner harbour. Work proceeded in two shifts, 6 a.m. to 2 p.m. and 2.p.m to 10 p.m. The widening of the west pier and folly commenced at the same time.

The summer fishing was poor and its total value for all Scots boats was down by £100,000. More drifters were fishing at Shields and coming home at the weekend, landing small catches at Anstruther on Saturdays. Not since the middle twenties had so much activity been seen in the harbour during the summer, and it proved a great attraction for the visitors in August.

Because of the Coffer Dam, many of Anstruther's steam drifters were laid up for a week or two in St Monans when preparing for the Yarmouth fishing, and after the Yarmouth fishing many of the local bauldies were laid up at St

Andrews. The Coffer Dam was eventually blown up in December. In the same month, St Monans had an addition to its fleet with the launch of the motor boat *Procyon,* 53 ft. long, at St Monans.

1938

There were now only nineteen steam drifters belonging to Anstruther and four belonging to St Monans, whereas in 1932 the corresponding figures had been thirty-two and seven, with four in Pittenweem. Pittenweem's last one disappeared from the records in 1937. This was a year when the receipts were likely to be more accurate than total landing figures as, unfortunately, much dumping of herring took place. This being the first year that the deepened inner harbour was in use, there was some difficulty in mooring boats at the west pier of the inner harbour, as they had had to reinforce the quay with a sloping projection at the bottom. Until the mud gathered, as it is today, the drifters used 12″ thick fenders to lie there when grounded.

On January 25th, there was a celestial phenomenon visible in every part of the country. Such a display of Aurora Borealis, I personally have never seen since. I quote, 'The scene was constantly changing and a large area of the firmament was often aflame with a blood red tinge.'

There was certainly stormy weather the following week, but nothing as serious happened for the rest of the winter as many of the older sages had forecast from the omens of the sky.

Only moderate catches prevailed until February 23rd, when the first 1,000 cran landing in Anstruther, and 500 in St Monans, was greeted by a slump in prices to the limit of 15s. per cran. The local committee thereupon decided to close the ports for two days. The next week saw a good average fishing, but on March 8th, there was a 3,000 cran total in Anstruther and 500 in St Monans and 600 in Pittenweem. This again reduced the price to the limit of 15s. and the port was closed again for one night. March 10th, saw 2,100 crans in total in Anstruther, 600 in St Monans, 400 in Pittenweem and again the ports were closed.

March 16th saw a 1,500 crans total in Anstruther, 500 in St Monans and the ports closed for two days, prices slumping to 12s. per cran.

Many good catches were made at that time:-

Ring Net:- *Floreat* (AH) 100 crans, *Volunteer* and *Launch Out* 84 crans, *Amber Queen* and *Floral Queen* 139 crans.

Anchored Net:- *Ivy Leaf* 35 crans, *Briar* 22 crans.

March 22nd saw a 1,300 cran total with many crans dumped back into the sea and again the port was closed. March 24th also saw many catches dumped and yet again the port was closed. Only 500 crans were disposed of and 1,000 crans were dumped. March 30th saw 900 crans bought for home markets and 600 crans dumped. There followed a week of diminished returns and no dumping, but on April 12th, there was more dumping and the port was closed, even though many of the stranger boats had gone home.

April 15th saw a 350 cran total and after that the fishing closed.

A maximum number of two hundred and seventy boats (sixty steam drifters and two hundred and ten motor boats) landed a total of 43,880 crans valued at £47,394 for the District, 27,000 at Anstruther, 10,000 at St Monans, 3,358 at Pittenweem, 1,314 at Crail and the rest at Methil.

Methil was used by the larger steam drifters on the neap tide weeks. Catches were up during the summer and at Yarmouth, but prices were poor and there were many limitations put on the fishing.

The St Monans Fleet lost a man, Robert Smith, at Yarmouth and many were fortunate to cover their expenses. This was the first year that the share fishermen qualified for unemployment relief. Signs of the impending War appeared locally with the banning of visitors to the Isle of May by the Admiralty. The last launch at Cellardyke harbour took place when Forbes launched the *Refleurir* 56 ft. by 18 ft., for A. Muir of Cellardyke. She had a 132 H.P. Kelvin diesel engine.

1939

In this the last full winter herring fishing before the start of World War II the full tally of fishing boats belonging to the District, starting at Buckhaven and moving eastwards was:

Buckhaven Three motor boats of less than 30 ft. in length

Methil & Leven Twelve motor boats of less than 30 ft. in length

Largo Three motor boats of less than 30 ft. in length

St Monans Three motor boats of less than 30 ft. in length, three steam drifters and thirty-one motor boats exceeding 30 ft. in length

Pittenweem Sixteen motor boats less than 30 ft. and seventeen motor boats exceeding 30 ft. in length

Anstruther Sixteen steam drifters, ten motor boats exceeding 30 ft. and two of
   less than 30 ft. in length
Crail Twelve motor boats less than 30 ft. in length
St Andrews Five motor boats less than 30 ft. in length
Tayport Two motor boats less than 30 ft. in length.
   There were also twenty-three registered sailing yawls under 30 ft. in length
in the District (my family having one of them).

Only eighteen steam drifters prosecuted the fishing this year, compared
with sixty the previous year, while one hundred and eighty-seven motor boats
appeared, compared with two hundred and ten in the previous year.

The year opened with prospects of a better foreign market, but January
went by without any day's total exceeding 100 crans. February's best day's
fishing was the 14th when a total of 780 crans were landed in Anstruther, 330
coming from the ring net, the best shots being *Spes Aurea* 55 crans and *Lothian
Queen* (LH) 40 crans, prices 20s.-35s. St Monans had 500 crans that day, with the
Carmania landing 40 crans.

February 28th saw heavy landings by the ring net boats. A morning's total of
2,100 crans was added to by the ringers landing another 600 crans in the
afternoon, caught in the daylight. The drift net boats only contributed 400
crans to the day's total of 2,700 crans, prices 20s.-25s.

The best shots were:- *Famous* (INS) 110 crans, *Gratitude* (LH) 100 crans, *Ben
Venuto* (AH) 100 crans and *Spes Aurea* 60 crans.

The same day St Monans had 400 crans with no ring netters being allowed to
land. The best shots were *Providence* with 70 crans and *Paragon* with 60 crans.

March 2nd saw a 1,400 cran total in Anstruther, prices 18s.-19s. March 3rd
had a 720 cran total with the steam drifter *Pilot Star* having 100 crans and *Floreat*
(AH) 100 crans. March 7th saw a 1,730 total in Anstruther, 1,500 for ring net,
prices 18s.-23s. The best boat was *June Rose* (LH) with 100 crans. St Monans had
a 300 cran total that day, the best shot being *Deo Volento* with 58 crans. March
9th saw 1,300 total at Anstruther, prices 18s.-20s. 6d. After that the fishing
gradually declined. With fewer boats and the fishing more spread out, the
fishermen were spared the disappointment of dumping herring, which had
probably been the cause of the smaller fleet. The maximum number of boats
was two hundred and five (eighteen steam drifters and one hundred and
eighty-seven motor boats) landing a total of 42,308 crans valued at £52,254 for
the District, 28,000 being landed at Anstruther, 10,000 at St Monans, 1,400 at
Pittenweem, 956 at Crail and the remainder at Methil. War was declared
before the jetty was built at Anstruther, but the work proceeded and so
Anstruther now had a beautiful harbour for the winter herring, just as it was
about to disappear.

A nobbie being launched broadside on at Cellardyke harbour.

1940

All the local steam drifters along with fifteen motor boats were requisitioned by the Admiralty and although many of the local people I talked to refused to believe that there was any drift net fishing during this, the first winter herring of the War, the figures are in the Fishery Office: Twenty-six steam drifters, sixty-six motor drifters and ninety-two ring net boats prosecuted the fishing, the steam drifters all being from the Moray Firth. This was confirmed from St Monans as their motor boats *Annie Mathers, Lively Hope* and *Elspeth Smith* were engaged in the drift net at the winter herring fishing, and they were only allowed to fish to the east of a line from the May Island to a buoy off Cellardyke. They were herded into this area by an armed trawler. The landings at Anstruther were 20,000 crans, at Pittenweem 5,000, at St Monans 3,000 and at Crail 378 crans. The total for the District was 29,378 crans valued at £124,693.

1941

Very little is known of the fishing in this year. There were certainly no steam drifters and no fishing in the dark, so only the ring net and anchor net fishing produced the landings, the total for the District being 15,968 crans of which Anstruther had 8,750 crans.

1942

This was the most remunerative year in the history of the winter herring, all herring being caught in the daylight, as was to happen for the rest of the War. The landings at Anstruther were 19,000 crans, at Pittenweem 6,500, St Monans 1,500 and Crail 126, making a total of 27,282 crans for the District from ninety-one boats, giving the record return of £134,414.

1943

This year saw the start of the final decline, more rapid than anybody could have expected. Most of the eighty-three motor boats engaged in the fishing were ring net boats, which landed 2,900 crans out of the total for the District of 3,546 crans valued at £18,191. Of this, 2,000 crans were landed at Anstruther, 1,100 at Pittenweem and 300 at St Monans. Only one redeeming factor can be mentioned. There was an increase of 500% of white fish landings and now the seine net had become the main tool of the local fishing industry.

1944

There is nothing to mention about this year but the bare facts. The landings at Anstruther were 2,164 crans while Pittenweem and St Monans had 900 crans each, making 4,046 crans valued at £18,837 for the District. This was the last year that the motor yawl *Briar* of Pittenweem went to the anchor nets. As far as can be ascertained, this was the last boat to go to the anchor nets from Pittenweem.

The *Gratitude,* ML 17, skipper A. Wood of Pittenweem and the *Good Design,* KY 115, skipper J. Watson of Pittenweem landing a catch of herring from the ring net. (from a painting by More Horsburgh)

1945

During this year St Monans had fourteen fishing boats, ten of which were over 30 ft.; Pittenweem had twenty-two, fifteen of which were over 30 ft.; Anstruther and Cellardyke had sixteen, of which seven were over 30 ft.; and Crail had twenty-one, all under 30 ft. In the whole District from Buckhaven to Crail there were still thirty-nine sailing vessels. The fishing during this year was very poor, but it was the last time that the total exceeded 1,000 crans. 18 crans were landed in St Monans, 800 in Pittenweem, 1,000 in Anstruther and 80 in Crail. The total for the District was 1,961 crans valued at £9,044.

Now that the War was over it was announced in July that echo sounders would now be available for fishing boats.

1946

The first steam drifter to try the winter herring fishing after the War was the *Tyrie,* a Peterhead registered boat on loan to skipper John Gardner of Cellardyke, with a local crew. A few bauldies were available to try the drift net, but they fished without success, the best catch being only 12 crans. The anchor net and ring net were also failures. St Monans had 2 crans, Pittenweem 10, Anstruther 82 and Crail 10, giving a total of 94 crans, valued at £431, the lowest ever recorded.

Where there had been eighty-three vessels over 35 ft. before the war, now there were only forty. Before the year finished, the steam drifters *William Wilson* and *Cosmea* returned from the War.

Among the new boats launched locally before the end of the year were the *Good Design II* for Pittenweem, built at St Monans, and the *Golden Arrow* for Cellardyke. The steam drifter *Tyrie*, with a local crew, shared £365 per man at Yarmouth.

1947

This can be marked down as the year that finished the winter herring fishing, although there were spasmodic landings of herring on odd occasions during the following few years.

The fishing fleets might have been expected to make a special effort after the War, but they never got the chance. No one who lived through this winter can ever forget it. The wind swung between east-south-easterly and south-easterly for weeks, drifting into months, in the early part of the year. The Siberian anti-cyclone blocked the roads with snow, and the sea and sky in the sea-mouth were of a greeny-grey colour, the like of which I have never seen again.

Not until April was the first cran landed in an East Fife port, and that was at St Monans, and only 69 crans were landed in the District, 56 of them in Anstruther. This was the year when the last anchored net was shot in the District, by the *Comely* of Crail.

In March, the motor boat *Hope* was launched for D. Wood of Pittenweem and she was the first local boat to be fitted with an echo sounder, which was installed by McKenzie & Spark.

Among other new boats launched in the District were the *Minnie Wood, Guide Us* and *Guiding Light,* all for Pittenweem. Only half a dozen local boats went to Great Yarmouth, a shadow of the fleet of fifty or so that used to go south. They were *Wilson Line, Cosmea, William Wilson, Cold Snap, Taeping* and *Irene Julia.*

1948

Most of the local boats left to fish on the west coast. The few who remained to fish for herring in the first three months of the year landed a total of only 27 crans, 9 of them in Anstruther. In Parliament questions were asked about this disastrous situation and the Fishery Office's Research Vessel *Clupea,* had only 30 herring for its biggest catch while using drift nets about the May Island. The

Part of the Herring Fleet waiting to enter Anstruther harbour.

examination of their catches showed that stocks were unusually low for fish spawned in 1940 to 1942. At East Anglia, the *Wilson Line*, KY 322, was runner up for the Prunier Trophy.

1949

This year saw a total of 74 crans for the District and 51 crans in Anstruther. Not more than a dozen boats tried for herring and those belonged mainly to St Monans. The Research Vessel *Clupea* also tried again and the scientists found that the few large herrings that they caught resembled the herring found off Shetland. At Yarmouth the *Refleurir*, only 56 ft. long, had 160 crans after giving away some nets to another boat which got 80 crans from them.

1950

Half a dozen St Monans bauldies comprised the last of the East Fife winter herring fleet, but the few herring they caught were used mainly for bait for the great lines. Apart from these, the catches were mainly of two year old summer halflin herring. The total catch for the District was given as 12 crans with Anstruther blank. The local boats at Yarmouth had a better year and the boats and skippers were:

Taeping (H. Bett), *Irene Julia* (J. Bett), *Refleurir* (A, Muir), *Noontide* (J. Brunton), *Coriedalis* (P. Gardner), *William Wilson* (James Wilson), *Wilson Line* (James Muir), *Integrity* (R. Mackay), *Carmania* (J. Smith.) (The *Coriedalis* was the former *Cosmea.*)

1951

Thirty boats working fron Newhaven landed halflin herring at Newhaven, average size 550 to a basket. They were sold for fish meal. The only local landings were in St Monans. In mid-January, 20 crans were landed by the St Monans boats, *Carmania, Providence* and *Paragon*. They sold at £6 12s. per cran. This was the last mention of the winter herring locally. Only 1 cran was landed in Anstruther, 3 in Pittenweem and 47 in St Monans.

The last figures available from the Fishery Office are for 1954, when 400 crans were landed from ring net boats. The herring were caught between the Carr and the Tay. They were not winter herring, but immature summer herring. During the fifties, catches of sprats and immature herring were landed in the local ports and loaded into lorries in bulk for fish meal. Right up to the early sixties, some of the St Monans bauldies continued to ply their drift nets in the upper reaches of the Firth, three of them being *Integrity, Winaway* and *Paragon*. The last named was probably the last East Fife boat to shoot drift nets for herring, as she continued to go regularly to the drift net at Peel in the Isle of Man until 1976. Meanwhile, the Yarmouth fishing had also gradually faded away. The last steam drifter from East Fife to go to Yarmouth was the *Coriedalis*, KY 21, skippered by James Muir, in 1956. He returned the next year in his new motor boat *Silver Chord*, KY 124, to become the first local winner of the Prunier Trophy for her top shot for the season of 212 ⅓ crans.

Winter herring are still landed in small amounts by the seine net in the winter herring months of January to March each year, but the days of the anchor net and drift net fishing are over. Should any shoals ever appear again, they would soon be swallowed up by the ring net or purse seine net, but that is another story. As one story came to an end, another began with the opening of Pittenweem Fish Market and the beginning of the local prawn fishing towards the end of 1954.

Appendix I

The following verses were written by my Father

THE HERRIN'

(Written in 1937, when the Winter Herring Fishing was at its height)

The shades o' nicht were drappin' fast.
When oot o' Anster Harbour passed
A fleet o' craft o' various sort,
A' keen tae catch—but no for sport—
The herrin'.

Cam' first a muckle steam steel drifter,
Twa wud anes followed at her quarter,
Then came the motors, auld and new,
Yet, a' bent on the self-same view,
The herrin'.

Their bold initials did proclaim
Their port o' registry or hame,
Frae Berwickshire, north past the Spey,
Frae Argyll Coast, frae Ballantrae,
For herrin'.

Cam' hame boats frae the Firth o' Forth,
Baith frae the south side and the north;
While mony a Scottish town and creek
Sent their flotilla—a' tae seek
The herrin'.

The sicht was bonnie, without doot,
Tae see them as they a' sailed oot,
Alert and skilfu' was each man,
Eager the slightest sign tae scan—
O, herrin'.

On ilka pier that nicht there stood
A cheery, jovial, motley crood;
Jokes were exchanged frae pier tae boat;
But yet, wan word drooned a' the lot,
'Twas herrin'.

"Try not the 'Hirst'," the veteran cried
The skipper smiled—then lood replied,
  "Your guid advice I hear, auld man,
Yet, there they congregate tae spawn,"
        The herrin'.

"And tho' baith time and tide are late
Doon there this nicht my nets I'll shate,
  My wife and bairnies, big and wee,
And a' my crew depend on me,"
        For herrin'.

The veteran saw them disappear,
Then daundered slowly up the pier,
  A smile lit up his face and broo,
While jist ae word escaped his moo,
        'Twas herrin'.

Appendix II

PETER MURRAY (REEKIE) His Book, Cellardyke 1866,
Carmi,—December 29th (KY 604)

1866

1st Fishing of 'Carmi'

July	27	¾ cran at £2 Mackerel 9s.	£ 1	19s. 0d.
	28	½ cran at £1 16s.		18s. 0d.
Aug	3	Mackerel		11s. 0d.
	4	2¼ cran at £1 15s.	3	19s. 0d.
	8	21¼ ⅛ cran at £1 11s.	32	18s. 0d.
	9	¼ ¾ Basket at 6s. 3d.		10s. 0d.
	10	2¾ cran at 34s.	4	12s. 0d.
	13	1¼ cran at 25s.	1	11s. 6d.
	14	9 ⅛ cran at 25s.	11	8s. 0d.
	15	½ cran at 24s.		12s. 0d.
	16	43 cran at 25s. 6d.	54	14s. 6d.
	28	2½ cran at 25s.	3	1s. 6d.
	30	2¼ cran at 26s.	2	18s. 6d.
Sept	15	13½ cran at 21s.	14	13s. 6d.
			£134	6s. 6d.
		Divided	£16	12s. 0d.
		Expenses	£18	2s. 6d.

1866

Carmi at Lowestoft

Total by end of November.

22L	1T	7H	£189 0s. 2d.
Divided			£12 10s. 6d.
Expenses			£101 13s. 8d.
With Rope			16s. 9d.

L = 1 Last = 10,000 Herring
T = 1,000
H = 100

1867

Choice

Feb.	19	1½ basket	9s. 0d.
	20	6½ cran at 29/-	£9 8s. 6d.
	21	13 cran at 22/-	£14 6s. 0d.
	23	8½ cran at 30/-	£13 5s. 0d.
	27	8¼ cran at £1-	£8 5s. 0d.
	28	10¼ cran at 10/-	£5 2s. 6d.
March	1	4¾ cran at 12/6	£2 19s. 0d.
	2	1 cran at 17/-	17s. 0d.
	5	1½ cran ¾ basket at 32/-	£3 13s. 0d.
	6	1¾ Basket	12s. 6d.
	7	2½ cran at 36/-	£4 10s. 0d.
	15	1½ cran at 17/-	£1 5s. 6d.
	16	8¼ ⅛ cran at 23/-	£9 9s. 0d.

Divided at Winter Herring £17 12s. 6d.

WINTER HERRING EXPENSES

Allowance At Elie	1s. 0d.
Train 2/-11d Coals 3/-8d Allowance 1/-4d	7s. 11d.
Allowance at Addy 1/-10d Dues 2/-	3s. 10d.
Sugar, Tea 5/- Lines, net 2/-6d Oil All 2/-	9s. 6d.
John Anderson Allowance 9/-9d Mr Young 4/-6d	14s. 3d.
Sugar, Tea 4/6d Nets driving 1/- Dues 2/-	8s. 0d.
Jar 6d	
Crail, Sugar, Tea, Dues 5/-3d Allowances 4/-6d Crew	
Allowance 2/-3d one Allowance 10½ d	12s. 10½ d.
Allowance 1/-9d Basket Selvage 5/- Dues 1/-	
Coals 2/-6d Sugar, Tea 1/- Nets 1/-6d	
Luckpenny 2/-6d Stores Week 6d	16s. 0d.

1875

Venus

February	2	3¼ crans ¾ basket at 50s.	£ 8. 10s. 0d.
	4	Herrings	16s. 6d.
	5	2 crans ¾ basket at 54s.	5. 17s. 0d.
	6	6¼ crans at 33s.	10. 3s. 0d.
			£25. 6s. 6d.

Expenses 27s. 6d. Divided £3

February	9	2¼ crans at 40s.	£ 4. 9s. 0d.
	10	1½ crans at 24s.	1. 16s. 0d.
	12	13½ crans at 16s.	10. 14s. 0d.
	13	1¼ ⅛ cran at 32s.	2. 2s. 0d.
			£19. 1s. 0d.

Expenses 11s. 6d. Divided £2 6s.

February	20	Herring	7s. 0d.
		Great Line shot	£19. 11s. 6d.
		15 cran at 26s. 6d.	£19. 15s. 0d.
			£39. 13s. 6d.

Expenses £3 1s. 6d. Divided £4 11s. 6d.

February	22	¼ ⅛ cran	£ 12s. 0d.
	24	3¼ crans at 35s.	5 7s. 6d.
	25	¾ ⅛ at 18s.	15s. 0d.
	26	½ ⅛ at 16s.	10s. 0d.
			£7 4s. 6d.
			(Discount 2s.)

Dues 4s. Allowance 12s. 6d. Tea 2s. 6d. Nets 1s. 6d. Divided 15s.

March	1	Herring	6s. 0d.
	2	1 cran at 28s.	£1 8s. 0d.
	3	Herring	3s. 0d.
			£1 17s. 0d.

Allowance 5s. Dues 3s. Tea 2s. 6d. Society 2s. 4d. Divided 3s.

March	9	¾ cran	£ 2 5s. 0d.
	11	¾ cran	1 4s. 0d.
	12	8 ¾ cran	14 0s. 0d.
			£17 9s. 0d.
			(Discount 4s.)

Dues 3s. Nets 1s. 6d. Society 1s. 4d.
Tea 2s. Allowance 6s. Fitting Great Line Ends 11s.
Divided £2

Winter Herring Fishing £14 15s. 6d.
This was exceeded in 1883 when they divided over £22

Appendix III

EXTRACTS FROM ARTICLES WHICH APPEARED IN THE EAST FIFE OBSERVER BY "AULD WULL" IN 1927. HE WAS WILLIAM SMITH, WHO WAS THE PORT MISSIONARY AT ST ANDREWS, RETIRING IN 1922.

Cellardyke 70 Years Ago

I was born there nearly 80 years ago, and lived in it till I was fourteen. I left then and I have lived for many years in its neighbourhood, but have not had my home in it since. I left, the year the railway came to Anstruther. The station was at West Anstruther then and long after, till the railway came to Crail, when it was removed to its present position.

On leaving to push my way in the world I went to the ticket office and asked a ticket for Leith. James Brown, who was the station master, asked me how old I was. I answered 'fourteen'. He said, 'You're no very big, we'll let ye for half a ticket.' He had been agent for the steamer *Forth,* which sailed three times a week between Anstruther and Leith. I suppose the railway company, by appointing him, thought they would capture the steamer's trade.

It is of the period prior to that I would like to give some reminiscences of Cellardyke—the late fifties and early sixties.

The principal fishing at that time was the Lammas herring fishing. I forget the exact dates at which this started. It was in July, nearer the end of the month than the beginning. Some of the boats went to fish for four or five weeks at Gourdon or Stonehaven. There was no Aberdeen fishing at that time; at least I never heard about it.

I went two years with my father to Stonehaven, I was ten years old the first year. The crew of the small boat without deck or bunk was my grandfather, my father, my uncle and two half dealsmen. The fishing ground was from five to fifteen miles out. My father only let me go to sea when it was good weather. On other nights I had to stay ashore in our lodgings with my aunt, who was cooking for the crew. One night our landlord, who often took me out to the handlines took me out to what we called the 'jigs' and I got a quantity of herrings on the 'jigs' which supplied the crew's breakfast next morning, they having got none at all in their nets. We usually fished four weeks at Stonehaven, then came to Cellardyke to be in time for the 'auld hakes'.

The first year I remember we left Stonehaven in the little boat at four o'clock and we got to Cellardyke at eleven. The wind was right aft, and we had two sails, and we set the one on the one tack and the other on the other tack. The boats fishing at home tried it for the first few weeks about the Bass and Law, in one ground, or between the May and the land in eighteen fathom water. They did very little for the first three weeks or so, their takes being a few crans. It was when the herring set inshore to spawn that they made their fishing. That was then their harvest-time. Sometimes two big shots at the Peffer Sands near Dunbar, or at the Craig off North Berwick, then at the Traith off Pittenweem, and then at the Auld Hakes. They got the herring then at the high and low water slack, both by night and by day. And if successful at these places a boat would sometimes get as much as three hundred crans in a week or ten days. At the Hakes and the Peffer Sands the nets were anchored, but in the Traith and the Craig they were set at the float.

I remember one year at the Craig about forty fleet of nets got into a bunch and most of them were rendered useless. At the Traith, they fished with long tows, letting the nets drift over the ground, and in shooting the nets they had to shoot them so as to be over the spot where the herring were when the tide turned, for it was then the herring swam. I do not know whether it was the case or not, but I heard it said that the herring were lying with their noses sticking in the sand and when the tide turned, then they turned too, and it was then they were caught. The first time I remember being at the fishing was when I was eight years old and my father took me with him in his boat to the fishing in the Traith. It was during the day and as we were unsuccessful, and the boat was not coming in but was to remain out and try it the next tide, and there being no sleeping accommodation in the boat, I was put onboard another boat and sent ashore. I was landed at Cellardyke by John Brown, his partner being his son-in-law, Andrew Henderson, who was some years after that the king fisher of Cellardyke. I remember my father always fished better in the Hakes than the Traith. Whenever the Crail men saw the herring had set into the Hakes they sent word to Cellardyke, and through the town the cry was raised 'Herring in the Hakes'.

Immediately all was excitement and bustle, and a rush made to the fishing ground at once. At these places, and especially the Hakes the boats were filled as full as they could hold with herring, and the ballast and some of the gear were put ashore so that the boat might carry as much as possible. I remember on one occasion on a Sunday when the news came to the town that there were 'herring in the hakes' but as the Cellardyke men would not fish on Sabbath, none of them loosed a rope until after twelve o'clock on Sabbath. My father went out early on Monday morning and shot a fleet of ten nets. Thinking the tows were too long they were about to go along the fleet of nets and shorten the tows when they discovered that the herring were already in the nets and so they hauled them in and were up at Cellardyke harbour with forty-six crans by ten o'clock in the morning. In leaving the fishing ground they anchored a fleet of ten nets further out. After discharging their morning's shot, they returned and hauled the nets they had left, and were up at Cellardyke before ten at night with seventy-five crans. That was good work for a Monday. The seventy-five cran was as much as the boat could carry. They used to fill the boats as full as they could hold, sinking them up to the number forward and up to the name aft in the water. I have known them so full coming across the Dunbar grounds, and a bit of wind from the west meant that they had to throw some of the herrings overboard, to lighten the boat. There was once a boat so loaded at the Hakes that as soon as she got round the Carr the westerly sea filled her and she sank with the result that a man and a boy were drowned, the rest of the crew being saved by some of the boats that were near.

The nets at that time were put out to dry every day, and every crew required to have net ground for that purpose. The mill park used to be let by roup every year for this purpose before the fishing began. My father had his net ground in what we called William Fowler's park, which was where the houses at Burnside are now. When the boats were engaged in fishing night and day at the time in places I have mentioned, the women spread the wet nets and had them dry on the return of the boats. They did not need to shoot many nets at these times. The boats were engaged to fishcurers and each fishcurer had his distinctive mark on the mast of the boat engaged to him. There were a number of fishcurers at that time both in Cellardyke and Anstruther. The boats engaged to the Cellardyke curers usually discharged their herrings in Cellardyke, while those of the Anstruther curers landed theirs at Anstruther.

Since that time great changes have taken place in the fishing industry as in everything else. I do not think anyone at that time anticipated the time when Cellardyke fishermen would be prosecuting their calling in steam drifters. Steam ships were then in their infancy. I heard an old fisherman say, the first time he saw a steamer coming down the Firth that he thought it was a ship on fire. I remember the first channel fleet of the Navy which I saw, were beating down under sail. They had auxiliary steam but were not using it. A pretty sight it was. The fishing boats at that period were all open. The first improvement was a small cabin forward called a bunk. The first boat with a bunk that I saw was the *Choice* belonging to James Murray. Then they got a bit of a deck from the bunk to the main thwart. The boats at that time carried two sails and a jib. The foremast was stepped at the fore thwart, and the main mast at the main thwart. The main sail was usually bigger than the fore sail. Although the boats were smaller in those days, they carried when line fishing eight of a crew, and when the boat put about, four men tacked the foresail and four the mainsail. When engaged in herring fishing they only carried a foresail and sometimes a jib, the herring fishing being mostly inshore. They had no floor, they had what was called bottom boards. The ballast was composed of pavement stones built on top of each other under the main thwart. I think that later some of the boats had ballast boxes filled with stones in the same place. The boats at that time were not painted but tarred. It was easy to distinguish a new boat from an old one then. The new boat was lighter colour whereas the old was darker. They were scraped and tarred once a year at least. We boys at that time could distinguish the boats miles away. We could tell by some mark such as a new yard, new mast, new cloth in sail, rake of yard etc., what boat it was. We could also tell whether the boat had a good catch of fish by her weight in the water. The herring nets were made of hemp, not of cotton as at present. The winter herring nets were white and preserved by being dipped in alum, while the summer herring nets were black. They were barked with the bark got from the tan work. There was a tan work belonging to a Mr Dairsie, situated in the East Green. It was said, I do not know whether it was the case or not, but I have heard that the previous proprietor of the tan work was an old man who sold the concern to Mr

Dairsie on condition that he was to pay a certain sum weekly, as long as he lived. I suppose the weekly sum would be sufficient to keep him. However he did not live long, so that the buyer got a bargain of the work.

The nets then were not so long or so wide as in use now but they were bulkier. Before the days of net factories they were wrought by hand. I remember I had, when I came from school, to braid eight rounds every night—that was, I had to work eight rows of meshes as my nightly task and sixteen on Saturday. Sixteen meshes was half a yard. I generally had one done about the New Year when as a reward, my mother made 'clack'. It was made of treacle—a treat to us boys. There were no chocolates or so many sweets to be had then as there is now, and we had not the money to buy it, if there had been.

At the end of the herring fishing all the boats that were not needed for the winter line fishing were laid up, most of them not to come down again till the next Lammas fishing, the others to be launched at the winter herring. A few were laid up on a piece of ground at the upper end of the west pier at Anstruther harbour, a few at Cellardyke harbour, but most of them were laid up at the town's green. They usually lay in three tiers. The upper tiers contained the boats that would not be used till the next year's fishing, while those required for the winter herring occupied the lower tier. Before being used again, they, after being cleaned and scraped, had a fresh coat of tar. The letters before their numbers were AR. Some years after, they were changed to KY. To get the boats to the town's green they were put on two pairs of iron wheels fastened by chains to each other, and to the boat, and they were hauled up the slip out of the harbour by the men turning a capstan round which wound a chain, and when the boat was up the street, she was pulled by horses and later still, traction engines were used for that purpose, but at the period of which I am writing, the fishermen did the job themselves. There were one or two outside stairs on the road, and now and then the stairs would be damaged by the boat on wheels passing along the street and coming against the stairs. We boys waited to watch when the men were not looking and climb up the chain at the side of the boat by which she was fastened to the wheels, and get aboard and have a ride. There were sometimes accidents, both in hauling up the boats and launching them again: These usually happened in putting the boat in or taking her off the wheels. If I recollect right, I think one man was killed. I know, at any rate, some were seriously injured. I remember that on one occasion I and another boy called James Barclay got up on the top of the capstan while the men were unwinding the chain that was round it causing it to spin round rapidly Very soon we both got giddy and fell off. I had fallen first and had hit my head on an iron roller, and was rendered unconscious. I came to myself some hours later in my granny's bed, I had been carried to her house which was close to hand. My companion had been more fortunate as he fell on top of me and escaping unhurt, got up and ran.

After the herring fishing there came the winter line fishing. There was no English fishing at that time. The coals used in Cellardyke and Anstruther came by sea before the days of the railway, so at the close of the herring fishing these men would go in a fishing boat to St Davids or Wemyss for fifteen tons of coal which they divided amongst them. A number of the fishermen were members of the Naval Reserve, and they found this the most convenient time to put in their drill in the training ship at St Margaret's Hope. The line fishing lasted from about the beginning of October to nearly the New Year. The boat went to sea every day when the weather was favourable, going out the one tide and returning the next. The common thing was to bait six 'taes' of line to a man—that was forty-eight to a boat. The bait used was chiefly mussels from Newhaven or Port Glasgow. Sometimes when the mussels were scarce limpets were used. Many times, as a boy, I along with others had to go among the rocks as far as Caiplie and the Coves, gathering limpets. We also used to go up the country and gather grass by the side of the road and fields, which we brought home and spread out to wither, then it was used to lay the layers of baited hooks on when baiting the lines. During the line fishing the boats used Anstruther harbour more than at Cellardyke, although some of the boats frequented the latter at times, especially when there was little wind and the men had to use the oars to propel the boat. I remember when it was dark, when the boats were coming into the harbour we boys would be at the end of the little pier, and as we heard a boat coming in we would shout out 'what boat is that?' and if it was our father's we would hurry home and tell our mothers, and they would carry the lines they had baited that day to the boat and bring home the ones for the next day's baiting. When the boats came into Anstruther it was the custom for the wet lines to be put into a cart along with the kits. The kits were what each man kept his bread in. The youngest fisherman was sent along with the cart to show the carter where the members of the crew dwelt, so each man's lines and kit were put down at his door and on the cart's return it took the baited lines to the boat. So if a fisherman's lines were not baited when the cart came, they had to be carried to the boat afterwards.

If it was an early tide for the boats to go out, then they were back early and I remember my mother used to rise about four o'clock in the morning to get her lines baited in time, and as I was the oldest of the family, I had to rise too and help her to shell the mussels. I have seen her when she had a baby in the cradle, with the cradle string tied to her foot rocking the cradle and with her hands baiting the line. If the boats came into Cellardyke harbour, the lines were carried to and from the boats. Besides the fishermen's there were dozens of cadgers' carts that came to buy the fish. There was one that came regularly from as far as Perth. I think Stewart was the name.

The winter herring began about the New Year and lasted till March. I do not know the exact number of boats that were engaged at the fishing. I think perhaps about forty at the line fishing, and sixty or seventy at the winter herring fishing. The herring boats had six of a crew, four with nets and two half dealsmen. Then there were a number of boats from Buckhaven, Fisherrow, Prestonpans and other places. As this was the only place where winter herring was prosecuted at that time, a large number of buyers came from England, and the competition between them and the local buyers was in the fishermen's favour as it kept up the price. When the herring began to get scarce about the end of March, the great lines were put in, and the great line fishing commenced, the great lines being baited with herring. Then when the herring was done, the haddock lines were baited, and the haddocks used to bait the great lines with. It was the largest boats that were used for the summer lines and great lines. Many of the boats after the herring bait failed did not always use the haddocks to bait the great lines, but when they got a good shot of haddocks they came to the harbour with them and sold them. Two trips a week were made to the lines if the weather was favourable but only one trip was made to the great lines. (Note: 1 great line = 6 taes of 75 fathoms each, and had 115-120 hooks). Of course, they went further out to sea and baited more than double the hooks for the summer lines than they did for the winter lines. At the winter lines the haddocks were sold by the dozen, but in summer when they had bigger catches they were sold by the hundred. They were divided into classes—big and small. In later years they came to be sold by the hundred weight which was the better way, and when sold by the old, buyer and seller did not always agree to which were large and which were small.

At that time the boats did not carry side lights, nor do I think at a certain time in the fifties they had riding lights when at the nets. I think, they used to carry a choffer fire on the main thwart. I remember I was taken out to the fishing at Dunbar when I must have been very young, and there I saw lots of boats with these fires burning. I believe at one time ships did not carry side lights and I have heard of a boy on board a Coldingham steam boat, the first time he saw a ship's side-light, whether it was the green light or the red light that he saw, I do not know—but when he saw it he cried to the man who was steering, 'Doon wi' your helm or we'll be ashore for there's the light of the chemist shop right ahead.'

In my description of the herring fishing of that time I omitted to state that the herring nets were floated by bladders, chiefly cows' bladders, I believe. They were tarred, inside and out, and painted. There was no messenger in use for the nets. The head rope was pretty strong, and the bladders were attached to it. I may also state here that in the early sixties the fishing changed. The inshore fishing fell off, and the boats had to go further afield to seek for herring. The boats were larger, the smaller ones got out of use. The last two years I was at the fishing—1863 and 1864 were poor years. My father had a bigger boat then, and I went a summer in her. There were no engagements, the herring being sold at the day's price, and the boats were not confined to any port. We fished at Montrose for years, mostly at the 'White Spot' off Montrose. Any herrings we got we sold at Arbroath or Montrose, and sometimes at Anstruther. Our highest shot was sixteen cran and our total catch for the season would be about sixty, I think we would have about £8 to a hand. The prices were good owing to the scarcity of herring. The next year was somewhat similar. But that year, after the fishing was done, and the half dealsmen had gone away, the herring set in at the old 'Haiks.' The fishermen made up crews among themselves and during the week made more than they had done for the whole of the two years. I think only once since then have the herring been in such abundance in the 'Haiks'.

There used to be some exciting scenes at Anstruther harbour when the boats were taking the harbour in stormy weather. There were two channels—the west and the east. The steamer *Forth* which came from Leith generally took the west channel. I believe it was the deeper. Her berth was half way up the west pier. The steamer before her was called the *Zanthie*. I remember the first day the *Forth* came to Anstruther, there was a great crush on the piers to see her. She was a paddle boat and she took about three hours to do the passage to Leith. Her Captain was a Captain Albion. The boat usually came in through the east channel as it was the weathermost in easterly winds. I remember the first storm warning. It was, I believe, an Admiral Fitzroy who first issued these. At least we called them Admiral Fitzroy's storm signal. The boats had gone to sea that morning. I forget what month but it was the winter line fishing. They were caught in the storm and I remember that morning seeing them coming with bare masts. They were waiting for water in. At times they got out of sight down in the trough of the waves. I have heard my father say that when the sea took from them the May Light, there was too heavy a sea on to attempt the harbour. They were always loath, however, to run past their own harbour, and they often ran risks in coming in.

The custom was to lie till they saw a smooth, and then hoist up a sail and run in as fast as they could. And as we stood on the pier watching, we would utter such expressions as 'My, she's going to catch it; there's that range of breakers coming in astern of her,' and 'Ah, now she is all right, she'll be in before it.' That morning I wrote about the boats they all got in safely. The pier was crowded with women and children watching the boats taking the harbour, and there were some exciting scenes. To illustrate the difficulty and danger of taking the harbour in a storm let me mention the following:— 'One morning with the wind breaking from the northeast and a heavy sea on, the boats attempted the harbour. To sail the pier head they had to keep as far to windward in the east channel as they could. Some of them sailed the harbour mouth, and the men on the pier were ready to throw ropes to them and haul them safely in. Some of them did not sail the harbour, and in that case they dropped their anchor which had been prepared for such an emergency, and the anchor brought them up just at the edge of the breakers going in towards West Anstruther harbour. Those on the pier floated out bladders to which a rope was attached. The wind blowing from the pier to the boat took the bladder to the boat. The rope was hauled in by the crew, when the men, women and children on the pier head held on to it and pulled the boat to safety after she had slipped her cable. Many such scenes as these were witnessed seventy years ago. After this they got a cable and went with a rope to the assistance of the boats. I believe it was through some official of the Lifeboat Association seeing this that led to the placing of a Lifeboat at Anstruther.

Appendix IV

Winter Herring—January 1938

Monday, 10th

Day like summer, plenty sun. Went along to St Monans and rigged out our boat. Put in our ropes, bent mizzen and got everything ship shape. Mending nets till tea time.

Tuesday, 11th

Went to Anstruther, but very little doing. *Enterprise* 6 boxes sold at 16s. 3d. per box. Got chaff at Mill forenoon, mending during afternoon. Ordered 2 nets at A Cunningham's—60 yds 18 score at 35 rows 38 cotton.

Wednesday, 12th

Went to St Monans and took the boat up for coal. Two of us filled about 4 tons in bags. Left Methil about 8.30 p.m. and arrived in about 10 o'clock. *Taeping* 5½ crans, *Orion* 3½, *Enterprise* 1½. Put aboard 26¾ tons of coal. Got 2 nets along from Cunninghams.

Thursday, 13th

Took nets to boat and 'almed' them aboard. Set the nets down. Very few herrings. *Star of Hope* 1½ crans. *Good Hope* 1½ crans. Came home dinner time and tied 2 white nets on cork rope.

Friday, 14th

Not much herrings. *Taeping* 5 crans. *Liberty* 2 crans. *Argosy* 3 crans, £3. 5s. per cran. We came out at 1.30 p.m. shot about 4 o'clock. May Island bearing NW by W. Bass bearing W ½ S. Barns Ness SSW. *Plough* up at our tail. Wind from SE to SSE fresh with rain at times. *Royal Sovereign* and *Taeping* shot on our starboard quarter.

Saturday, 15th

Wind SSW. May Island bearing W ½ N about 2 miles from here. First shot 11 boxes at 11s. 6d. per box. A few of the bauldies with 2-3 crans. Came in at 12 o'clock. Lay at the middle pier.

Winter Herring—February 1938

Thursday, 10th

Called to watch 3.30 and out 4.30 a.m. A good morning this. May NW by N. Barns Ness SW. Bass W ½ S, tea watch. Turned out 4.30 wind W round to NW, very cold, got 2½ crans 52s. bought by Emmett, very few herrings, today 5 crans best shot. Came out at 11 o'clock, anchored in St Monans bight. Lifted anchor at 4 o'clock run off St Monans, shot, strong west wind very cold. May Island E by N. Elie NW by N. Called to watch 9.30 out 10.30. Wind NNW to NW. Like daylight with the moon.

Friday, 11th

Never had a watch after 10.30. Turned out at 4.30, had tea, started at 5.00, got 2½ crans, went to Methil and put herring out, got coal put in 15 tons 6 cwt. Left Methil 1.30 came down to the May, run South then shot the nets about 4.00, had tea 4.30, set the watch 5.00 out at 6.00. May Island NW ½ W. Bass W by S. Barns Ness S by W. Best shots in Anstruther today—*Breadwinner*. Best in Methil *Spes Melior* 5¼. Wind west fresh.

Saturday, 12th

Called to watch at 12.00 out at 1.00, moon bright, wind west moderate. Better fishing night. May WNW. Barns Ness S by W ½ W. Turned out 4.30, had tea, started at 5 o'clock, got 4 crans at 46s. 6d. Came in at 9 o'clock, lay at west pier, a lot of heaving to get up. A few 9-10 cran shots.

Monday, 14th

Went along and pulled down the nets. Home after 10 o'clock, looked over black net. Had dinner, went along and got out 2 o'clock. Shot nets about 4 o'clock, tea 5.00. May NW by N ½ N. Bass W by S. Wind East. Little bit swell but fine close. Watch 7.30 out 8.30. Full moon wind East light. May NW by N, Bass W by S. Looked on at 10.30 but not much doing, about score of herrings *Twinkling Star* pole *Mace* astern. *Acorn* into South of us next Barns Ness.

Tuesday, 15th

Watch at 3.00 out at 4.00. May N ½ W. Bass W ½ S. Barns Ness S by E. Turned out at 4.30, tea at 5.00 and started to pull, got 13 crans 22s.—Burgon. A few 10-15 cran shots but heavy fishing with ring net boats. Had spasm at pier end. Skipper hurt his hand with wheel. Too far into the Westward for going in. Spasm with herrings too. Thrown up by OS. OT. Came out at 3,00 p.m. Spoke Lucy, a few 10-20 cran shots inside of May. We shot Kellie over Pittenweem 26 fathoms. Called to watch 11.30 out 12.30 between May and Anstruther. Wind NE.

Wednesday, 16th

Turned out 4.30. Started to pull at 5.00, nets full of slime. Got 4 crans, went up to Methil. Not so many herrings today. Left Methil 2.30 very little appearance coming down. Came away South. Shot the nets about 5.00, tea at 6.00. Watch 8.30 out 9.30. May NW by N. Bass W ½ N. Barns Ness S ½ W. Wind E by N. Fine night, dull. *Clan*

Mackay berth North side. Boats well spread about. Best shots today, *Breadwinner* 14. *Wilson Line* and *Twinkling Star* 6. Saw the appearance off Pittenweem but did not have the faith to shoot.

Thursday, 17th
Turned out 1.30, tea, started to pull at 2 a.m. Got 6¼ crans at 22s. 6d. to D. D. Came along at 2.30. *Acorn* sprung a leak in harbour. Came out at 3.30. Shot nets about 4.30 wind NE by E. Elie Ness bearing NW ½ W. May East. Good fishing with bauldies. Watch 7.30 up till 9. Pittenweem NNW. May S by E. Started to pull at 11.30 pulled 18 nets for torch from NW. Had tea, started again got 23 crans at 22s. 9d. D. A. Macrae. Came out at 4 p.m., shot nets 4.30, tea 5, Kellie over West end of St Monans. *W Wilson* and *Twinkling Star* up at our tail. *Cosmea* berth off side of us. Watch 8.30, out 9.30. Wind NE by E. May E ½ S. Pittenweem N—21 fathoms water.

Nothing further mentioned that week.

Monday, 21st
Came along, set down the nets, went home and looked over black net. Dinner, turned in, had tea. Went along 4 o'clock. Shot nets at 5 SE May. Started to pull at 8.30. Went down to the ship. Shot away from the ship, swung up at 11.30. Ship bearing WSW wind, light from NE.

Tuesday, 22nd
Turned out 4 o'clock. Started 4.30 and got 3 baskets. *Twinkling Star* 45 in Leith. *Calli* 30 crans, one or two 20. Came out, made fast to *Quentia* off Anstruther. Shot nets Kellie over Mill in 14 fathoms. *Elspeth Smith* inside us and *A Mathers* outside us. Got 8 crans, put them in boxes at east pier. Went out and lay at May Island. *Storm Drift* came out, told us there was no fishing. Lifted anchor, sproules off Crail and Mill. Got in at 7.30 at night, lay west pier.

Wednesday, 23rd
Went along. Meeting with delegates, decided to close port. Arrived home at dinner time. Tied on cork rope on white net. Hung it out to dry.

Thursday, 24th
Went along. Meeting today decided to open port. Minimum price £1 a cran. Went along, but port remained closed.

Friday, 25th
Out at 11.30. Shot nets at 4.30. Tea 5. Wind S by W. Started to pull at 5.30 for shoal water 13 fathoms west side of Crail lights.

Saturday, 26th
All shot second time by 12 o'clock. May E by N. Elie Ness NW ½ W.

Monday, 28th

Came along, pulled down the nets went home about 9.00. West at 1, out about 2. A lot of appearance off the town. Shot next to the *Nor Ness*. *Twinkiling Star* berth inside us. *Three Bells* shot half along us at dark. Gave him the torch at 7 o'clock. May Island bearing SSW at 8 o'clock. Wind fresh from W. *Three bells* got pulled at 8.30 so put rope on starboard bow and pulled mizzen off.

Winter Herring—March 1938

Tuesday, 1st

Watch at 2 a.m. Wind still strong from W by S bearing May Island SW ½ W. North Carr N ½ W. March came in like the proverbial lion. Started to pull at 3.30, as wind went round to NW by W. Got 9¼ crans at 59s.—Mallett. Not a big fishing in Northesk at our pole. Got 14 crans. Came out at 3.30. Tea before we shot. Shot away from *Benison*. Next the May. Kellie over Hanna Harvie. May bearing SE. Started to pull at 11.30. Got torch from *Anchor of Hope*.

Wednesday, 2nd

8 tail nets foul, had to boat them. Got in and moored at 3 o'clock. Got 12¼ crans at 32s 6d.—W. B. Came out at 4. Lay at East side of May. Tea. Shot away from *Calli* at 6 o'clock. Watch 8-9. May Island SW by W. Carr NW ½ N. Fresh wind from WSW. Looked on at 12, took about 100 herring out of the first one. Slacked away again.

Thursday, 3rd

Turned out at 4. Tea. Started 4.30. Fresh wind the time of pulling, went to Methil. Got 5½ crans. A few 20 cran shots in Anstruther. Put aboard 12½ tons of coal. Got news of herring over at Barns Ness. Left Methil 3.30. Shot at 5 o'clock. Tea 5.30. Watch 6-7. Barns Ness S by W ½ W. Bass NW by W ½ W. *Carmania* inside of us. *Rambler Rose* to side of us. Wind W by S fresh.

Monday, 7th

Went along and set down the nets. Got out 4.30. Very little appearance down across the lights. Came west and shot. May bearing S ½ E at 6.30. Tea. Looked on at 9 o'clock. Two baskets out of the first two. Shot out again. May bearing SW by S. Carr bearing N. Started to pull at 10 for *Calli's* nets. Took in 24 bent on.

Tuesday, 8th

Turned out at 3.30. Got in at 6, lay at east pier. Got 25½ crans. First sale. Hold up on herring sales. Too many in, ring net boats full up. Meeting decided to close port. Went along at 11. Pulled up the nets. Home at 9.

Wednesday, 9th
Went along pulled down the nets. Mended a hole, pawed a pallet, got home at 11. Got out at 4.30. Shot nets, Kellie over the Kirks 20 fathoms. *Lucy Mackay* inside. *Mace* outside. Wind W fresh. Started to pull at 9. Got torch from *Calli* but *Lucy Mackay's* nets were along side of us. Got pulled at 11. 4 crans. Shot E side of May close to, May bearing W ½ N.

Nothing further written that week.

Monday, 14th
Went along at 1. A meeting on with committee so shifted out and lay at lighthouse. Got out about 3, not much appearance. So shot S of May. Barns Ness SSW. May WNW at 9 at end of my watch.

Tuesday, 15th
Watch at 3, made tea at 4. May NW by N. Bass W by S. Barns Ness W ½ W. Moderate wind SW by W. Got 5 ½ crans—Burgon 16s. Lay at west pier. Went out at 3 o'clock. Shot May about 19½ fathoms. Tea at 6. By that time we were the Lights in one. Wind SW by W fresh. Looked on at 11.30 intending to shift but *Plough* spoke us and said there were no herrings to west so bent on after we had pulled 6 nets.

Wednesday, 16th
Set watch at 12.30 out at 1.30. May SW by S. Started to pull at 2.30 so we set up on May. Got in just as the tide light was put out. Lay at east pier. Got 3 crans, 15s.—Bonthron. Ring net boats went out at 4 and were back at 6, full up so the port was closed. PD and BCK boats went away home in disgust.

Thursday, 17th
Port Closed.

Friday, 18th
Went out on Friday at 4. Steamed east side of Mây. Shot nets at 6. Tea at 7. May W by S. Watch at 11.30 out at 12.30. May SW ½ W. Wind SW light.

All for that week and that winter herring.

Wednesday, 30th
On way to great lines ....
Down at Carr at 7.30, about a score of ringers working near the beacon up till 11 o'clock. Steering NNE for Aberdeen.

Appendix V

WINTER HERRING LAMMAS DRAVE

Year	No. of Boats	Crans for District	Value £'s	Anster's Crans	Price per cran for District	Anster's Crans	Crans for District
1854						34,000	68,000
1855	180	4,000		4,000		36,000	75,000
1856	200	3,400		3,000		7,000	16,000
1857	200	9,100		7,000		9,000	23,000
1858	190	10,700		6,000		33,000	70,000
1859	210	7,900		4,000		10,000	28,000
1860	215	13,900		8,000		38,000	83,000
1861	212	20,200		10,000		15,000	38,000
1862	270	15,300		6,000		14,000	28,000
1863	265	13,200		5,000		6,000	12,000
1864	230	7,200		3,000		14,000	31,000
1865	220	10,700		5,000		4,000	15,000
1866	220	10,800		5,000		4,000	8,000
1867	215	18,400		8,000		7,000	21,000
1868	224	18,200		10,000		6,000	13,000
1869	230	13,400		8,000		3,000	10,000
1870	235	6,600		4,000		6,000	10,000
1871	250	24,900		12,000		1,900	5,000
1872	290	21,600		11,000		1,800	3,000
1873	250	9,600		4,000		2,000	4,000
1874	245	20,000		11,000		1,000	1,900
1875	240	8,700		6,000		230	280
1876	235	5,700		3,000		110	170
1877	220	2,500		1,400		1,500	3,000
1878	215	10,700		6,000		2,000	3,900
1879	200	2,100		1,500		5,000	6,000
1880	200	8,700		5,000		4,000	7,000
1881	245	17,000	30,000	11,000	1.76		2,000
1882	247	13,500		9,000			2,000
1883	239	13,900		9,000			8,000
1884	239	32,900		22,000			1,800
1885	220	36,900		25,000			2,000
1886	220	25,300		18,000			6,000
1887	176	32,400	13,000	25,000	0.40		4,000
1888	188	25,400	12,200	20,000	0.48		2,000
1889	169	19,300	10,000	15,000	0.51		2,000

Year	No. of Boats	Crans for District	Value £'s	Anster's Crans	Price per cran for District	Anster's Crans	Crans for District
1890	143	6,300		5,000			500
1891	123	7,900		6,000			1,000
1892	111	5,500		4,000			3,000
1893	101	24,300		21,000			3,000
1894	99	10,900		7,000			1,000
1895	90	6,800		5,000			3,000
1896	87	9,300		7,000			1,000
1897	146	12,600		10,000			500
1898	101	6,500		5,000			1,000
1899	91	20,100		15,000			1,000
1900	165	38,900		30,000			6,000
1901	268	39,100		30,000			7,000
1902	317	50,400	70,300	36,000	1.39		6,000
1903	285	32,600	32,700	23,000	1.00		5,000
1904	275	36,900	25,900	26,000	0.70		6,000
1905	250	39,200	31,800	25,000	0.81		5,000
1906	270	34,300	42,200	20,000	1.23		11,000
1907	245	29,600	38,800	16,000	1.31		13,000
1908	230	20,100	15,900	12,000	0.79		5,000
1909	220	8,100	8,700	3,000	1.07		7,000
1910	185	11,300	11,900	5,000	1.05		14,000
1911	186	15,500	12,400	7,000	0.80		8,000
1912	171	16,700	18,700	8,000	1.12		4,000
1913	194	8,900	12,200	3,000	1.37		5,000
1914	191	29,800	32,000	16,000	1.07		1,000
1915	N.A.	7,300	12,600	3,000	1.73		
1916	N.A.	2,200	11,400		5.08		
1917	N.A.	5,600	28,900		5.16		
1918	140	1,900	17,800		9.36		
1919	N.A.	5,000	31,600	2,000	6.32		
1920	102	4,100	12,500		3.05		
1921	109	24,900	48,700		1.96		
1922	93	4,300	11,500	4,000	2.67		
1923	92	7,800	9,300		1.19		
1924	126	12,300	19,900		1.62		
1925	91	10,400	12,400		1.19		
1926	143	12,100	19,600		1.62		
1927	105	14,900	14,200	7,000	0.95		
1928	112	26,500	28,500	13,000	1.08		

Year	No. of Boats	Crans for District	Value £'s	Anster's Crans	Price per cran for District
1929	168	27,000	42,900		1.59
1930	185	40,200	53,900		1.34
1931	173	21,900	42,300		1.93
1932	153	27,200	23,400	17,000	0.86
1933	160	31,200	36,700	18,000	1.18
1934	232	48,500	65,200	27,000	1.34
1935	275	58,300	72,600	34,000	1.25
1936	323	75,800	96,100	45,900	1.27
1937	313	36,000	65,900	21,000	1.83
1938	270	43,800	47,300	27,000	1.08
1939	205	42,300	52,200	28,000	1.23
1940	184	29,300	124,698	20,000	4.26
1941		15,900		8,700	
1942	91	27,200	134,414	19,100	4.93
1943	83	3,500	18,100	2,000	5.17
1944		4,000	18,800	2,000	4.70
1945		1,961	9,044	1,074	4.61
1946		94	431	82	4.59
1947		69		56	
1948		27	96	9	3.56
1949		74		51	
1950		12		—	
1951		51		1	
1952		34		6	
1953		158		152	
1954		400 Not winter herring but immature summer herring			

BREAK DOWN OF THE DISTRICT'S FIGURES FROM 1933-1940 (in Crans)

	1933	1934	1935	1936	1937	1938	1939	1940
Buckhaven	—	14	—	—	—	—	—	—
St Monans	9,078	14,526	15,572	18,856	8,066	10,020	10,692	3,382
Pittenweem	3,896	4,028	3,062	5,346	3,174	3,360	1,480	5,574
Crail	506	760	1,714	476	917	1,314	956	382
Methil	324	2,054	3,556	4,862	2,694	1,142	708	40
St Andrews	—	—	2	70	84	28	28	—
Tayport	—	—	—	320	62	—	—	—

Bibliography

LAMONT'S Chronicles of Fife (17th Century)
SIBBALD'S History of Fife 1710
LEIGHTON'S History of Fife (up to 1840)
1st STATISTICAL ACCOUNT 1799
2nd STATISTICAL ACCOUNT 1845
WOOD'S East Neuk of Fife 1862
JACK'S History of St Monans 1844
CHAPMAN'S Handbook to Elie and East of Fife 1892
GOURLAY'S Three books—1. Monks and Fishermen (about Cellardyke)
2. Anstruther
3. Our old neighbours
(written in the 1870's and 1880's)

Weekly Newspapers
Pittenweem Register (1844-1855)
East Fife Record (1855-1914)
East Fife Observer (1914-1967)

Statistics from Local Fishery Office.

Glossary

ANCHORED NET These were only used when the herring set in close to the shore and they were shot before the tide. There were usually five or six nets between anchors with eight to ten fathoms rope between a net and anchor.

ANSTER Anstruther. The town is divided by the Dreel Burn into West Anstruther and East Anstruther. Although written Anster it is pronounced Enster, the two parts being known locally as Enster Waster and Enster Aister.

AULD HAIKES An area half mile to one mile offshore between Fife Ness and Kingsbarns.

BARKING Nets could rot over a weekend if not preserved so they were dipped in a solution of cutch, for black nets. The corresponding method of preserving white nets was a solution of alum. When the East Fife fishermen changed from hemp nets to cotton nets they used linseed oil as a preservative, as they had done with the hemp nets. Unfortunately this made the cotton brittle when it dried out. A native who returned from the tropics told them that he had treated his cotton suits with alum water and this started the custom of treating the white nets with alum.

BARREL A unit of measurement used by some of the older fishermen until the 1940s. It was equivalent to a cran.

BARROW LIFTERS Hand barrows used to carry creels and nets. The lighter of the two persons carrying it went first and the stronger one took the rear as he carried more weight when going uphill.

BAULDIE A fishing boat of 35ft to 55ft length. Peter Anson mentions a Leith bauldie of 22ft, in his writings but it is generally agreed that 35ft is the minimum length for a bauldie and it would seem that what he was referring to was probably a 22ft yawl. According to the Scottish National Dictionary the name is derived from the Italian patriot Garibaldi. The first bauldies were converted from sail to be powered by 30 HP Kelvin paraffin engines. Later they were powered by diesel engines.

BEAM TRAWL A variey of trawl net in which a beam was used on the top of the net to keep the mouth of the trawl open, instead of the boards used today to open it from the side. Chains were put on the bottom to keep it down. The beam trawl was used mainly for catching flat fish.

BLUE STONE Copper sulphate. Some fishermen used this instead of cutch for barking their nets.

BOOM During stormy weather the boats in Pittenweem and Crail harbours were protected by wooden booms which were placed across the harbour mouth.

BOUNTY This was a subsidy offered by the government in the eighteenth century to encourage Scottish fishermen to compete with the Dutch who with their 'busses' exploited the North Sea from Shetland to the south-east coast of England. The bounty was withdrawn in 1829 but some of the curers kept the principle going to induce a fleet to fish exclusively for them. The sum was usually paid on striking a bargain to supply a set amount of fish at a fixed price.

BUCKERS Natives of Buckhaven.

BUSH ROPE The bottom rope, below the nets or sole rope. It was known in East Fife as the 'Messenger Rope'.

CADGERS Hawkers who went round the countryside with a horse and two wheeled flat cart selling 'caller herring'. One noted cadger in Crail who had only one hand, with a hook on the other arm, was crying his wares 'good cod roes' when he was stopped by a passer-by who asked him if there was much herring in Anster that day. 'Good Goad knows' he replied and then continued down the street calling his wares 'good Goad knows' instead of 'good cod roes'.

CALLER HERRING Fresh herring.

CHAUFFER FIRE A fire enclosed in an iron basket used in open decked boats. This type of fire was also used by coopers.

CONGESTED DISTRICT BOARD Originally set up in 1891 to help to create employment in overpopulated areas in Ireland, it was extended in 1897 to cover certain areas of Scotland.

CRAN $37\frac{1}{2}$ gallons of herring, measured in Scotland by four baskets, one basket being $\frac{1}{4}$ cran. During the two wars the fishery officer made his returns in cwts, with one cran being equivalent to $3\frac{1}{2}$ cwt. Today herrings catches are measured in tonnes, one tonne being approximately 5.6 crans.

CURING Herring for curing were gutted and salted then packed in barrels filled with brine. They were allowed to settle in the brine for at least eight days. The brine was then poured off and another two rows of herring added as shrinking would take place. The lid was fitted to the barrel and it was filled with fresh brine through a bung hole in the side. The bung was hammered home and the barrel was then said to be bung packed. It was then ready to be branded by the Fishery Officer as suitable for export.

CUTCH Catechu. It was bought by the hundredweight and steam heated in tanks into which were dipped the black nets.

DRAVE This was the name given to the summer herring fishing.

DRIFT NET A fleet of nets, any number between forty and eighty, a full size net being eighteen score meshes deep. This was too deep for the bauldies and they adopted a twelve score deep white net. Drift nets were shot before the wind.

DYKERS Natives of Cellardyke.

EAST FIFE AREA The area from Buckhaven to Tayport.

EAST NEUK The corner of Fife enclosed by a line drawn from Largo to Kingsbarns.

FARLANS The troughs into which the herring were put before the women gutted them for curing.

FIFIE Fishing boats with a vertical stem and stern. The largest was about 70 ft long and 21 ft broad and powered by a 60 H.P. Gardner paraffin engine.

FLEET The total number of nets shot by a boat was known as a fleet of nets. The bigger drifters would go with a fleet of seventy or eighty nets. Each member of the crew put in his share of the nets and they then drew cuts to see whose net was next to the boat in sequence so that if there was some misfortune it was a matter of chance whose nets were damaged. The rota would be altered according to individual arrangements.

FLUKE Flounder.

FOLLY Originally the name given to a wall built by a boatbuilder on the shore in front of the present Post Office in Anstruther. It was a foolish thing to do for it did away with a beach which absorbed the waves and provided a surface which reflected the waves and caused movement among the boats in the harbour. The name is now applied to the whole foreshore between Shore Street and the harbour.

GREAT LINES Known in England as long lines. Lines with large hooks for catching cod, skate, halibut etc. Before the Second World War the line was made of the best Italian hemp but since then a thicker sisal has been used. The line was made up of 6 taes with the hooks tied on at intervals of 3½ fathoms. The fathom was taken to be the distance between a man's hands when the arms were extended so there would be 115 to 120 hooks per line. A crew of seven men had 5 lines each so there would be over 4,000 hooks in a fully stretched fleet. Up to 1984 one East Fife boat still prosecuted the line fishing in the region of Faeroe. In East Fife the great lines were known as gartlins or gertlins.

HALF DEALSMEN Hired help in the fishing boats who were not owners of gear. They received only a half share of the profits unlike the regular fishermen who had their own nets or lines and so got one full share of the profits. Before the Great War many Highlanders and also miners from West Fife sailed as half dealsmen.

HALFLIN HERRING Immature herring, not old enough to spawn.

HANDLINES These were of three kinds, plus the Jigs. The sprouls were artificial fish with a pair of hooks embedded in the white metal of which they were made. If the hooks were loosely attached instead of firm they were known as rippers or murderers. In the month of June when the shore crabs were casting their shells they were used as bait instead of the sproules. Normally only two hooks were used on a handline and they were suspended below the lead sinker, at the end of the line. The mackerel season was July and August and these were caught on artificial flies of 15 to 17 haddock hooks on nearly invisible catgut, on a line with a lead sinker at the bottom.

HANNAH HARVEY A Cheltenham lady who gifted Anstruther its first lifeboat, *Admiral Fitzroy,* in 1865. Her interest in its activities gradually extended to embrace the local fishing community and she erected the lighthouse on Anstruther west pier to commemorate the centenary of the birth of Dr Thomas Chalmers. Although the lighthouse is officially known as the Chalmers Memorial Lighthouse it is generally referred to locally as the Hannah Harvey.

HIRST A rocky area of the seabed between the May Island and Crail which was a popular spawning ground for the herring. One of the guides to it was the guiding lights for Crail harbour in transit.

JIGS A method of catching herring on hooks. They were made from the wires that the women used for knitting. Three or four wires were attached at their mid points to a line so that when it was vertical the wires were horizontal. From the ends of each wire were suspended haddock hooks and at the end of the line was a lead moulded from an eggcup. The hooks were not baited as the idea was to hook the fish by jigging the line. They were used mainly in the summer and the best time for fishing was one hour before dusk and one hour before dawn. Often attempts to catch herring by net failed completely when the jigs were successful in the same area and then many old fishermen considered that the herring were seeing the nets and had 'too clear an eye' to be caught with nets.

KEELING SCALES Scales on the belly of the fish, in particular those between the vent and the pelvic fins.

LAMMAS Celtic autumn festival indentified with feast of St Peter ad Vincula, 1st August.

LAST A measure of herring used at Yarmouth and Lowestoft. Originally it was 10,000 herring but later was equivalent to 10 crans. The number of herring in a cran will vary according to the size of the fish and the winter herring in East Fife averaged about 1100 to the cran.

LINER The first steam fishing boats to be used in East Fife. They were found to be too big and clumsy for the herring fishing. They were superseded by the steam drifters.

LONG BANK A herring spawning area 40 miles east of the May Island.

NETS Up to the mid nineteenth century nets were made of hemp twisted into twine and had about thirty meshes to the yard. These were superseded by cotton nets, first made in Scotland at Musselburgh, and by the 1880s these were in universal use, the size of mesh varying from 34 to 42 meshes to the yard.

NOBBIE The Nobbie, or Nabbie, was the name given to the ring net boats which were generally varnished and had canoe shaped sterns. They ranged in size from 35ft to 55ft and were powered by diesel engines.

NUSSELS The local name for ossels. These were pieces of line about a foot long which were tied on to the top and bottom meshes of the nets and then used to secure the nets to the cork and sole ropes.

PARTAN The red, edible crab caught in the same type of pots as the lobster.

PAWLS Bollards on the pier for tying mooring ropes to.

PINING When herring were cured they were left to settle in barrels of brine for eight clear days. This operation was known as pining.

PORT DISTINGUISHING LETTERS A, Aberdeen; AH, Arbroath; BA, Ballantrae; BF, Banff; BCK, Buckie; CN, Campbeltown; FR, Fraserburgh; INS, Inverness; KY, Kirkcaldy; LH, Leith; ML, Methil; ME, Montrose; PD, Peterhead.

PRUNIER TROPHY A trophy donated by Mme Prunier of London which was awarded annually for the largest catch at Yarmouth or Lowestoft.

PUCKLE A small amount.

RAPES The plies of rope which went into the composition of the cork, or top, rope and the sole, or bottom, rope of the net.

RING NET A net shot in a circle by one of a pair of boats to ensnare a shoal of herring. When successful they often caught enough to fill both boats.

ROUP A public sale where the auctioneer accepted bids.

SEINE NET A net, lighter than a trawl, dragged along the bottom of the sea by a boat of moderate size. It can only be used on relatively smooth ground. The trawl required more hauling power as it was designed to be dragged over rough ground as well as smooth.

SHOT *v.* Past tense of shoot; the action of putting the nets into the sea from the boat. *n.* The catch. *e.g.* a shot of 20 crans.

SMA' LINES Sometimes called haddock lines, these were for catching smaller fish such as haddock and flounders. The hooks were usually of size 19 or 20 and were attached to the hemp line by plaited horsehair about 15in long, Cockenzie lines having a longer and thinner hair. The taes had 120 hooks, 3½ ft between each hook. In a crew of 5 men there would be 2 lines each of 6 taes, over 7,000 hooks per boat. The favoured bait was mussels, the Pittenweem men using Eden mussels or the softer, Tayport ones. In times of scarcity mussels were sometimes obtained from Wales or Kings Lynn. Herring was also used for bait, each herring being cut into 32 baits. In the summer, herring for bait was sent from Eyemouth. These herring arrived about 3.30pm and were hurried down to the homes, where the lines were baited and shot into the sea about 10pm.

SPENT Herring were spent after they had spawned. They were thin and brought poor prices at the market.

STEAM DRIFTERS The earlier, wooden steam drifter had a maximum keel length of 82 ft to 84 ft and was powered by a compound steam engine. The standard steel drifter had a keel of 86½ ft with an overall length of 92½ ft and a beam of 18½ ft to 19 ft. They were powered by triple expansion steam engines.

STOKER The engineers and firemen in the drifters were on weekly wages, but they were also allowed 2 taes of lines at the gartlins. the catch from this was known as stoker. In poor times this often appeared disproportionate to the share fishermen so they also demanded 2 taes each which was paid out clear of the expenses of the boat. Ultimately it was bargained away as the owners did not like it as they had no share of it.

TAES A taes was a measure of 75 fathoms of line.

TARRY An alternative name for cutch.

TREATH Also known as the Fluke Hole and California, this fertile fishing ground is about one mile off Pittenweem. The Anstruther and Cellardyke fishermen called it the Treath while it was, and still is, known as the Fluke Hole to the Pittenweem men.

TRUSS HOOPS Tough wooden hoops used to bind the wooden barrels.

TULLY Tiller for steering the boat.

TYING ON The operation of attaching the meshes of the net to the cork and sole ropes. They were attached by nussels about a foot long, which were tied about six to eight inches apart. This operation was very important for it affected the hang of the net which, in turn, affected its catching ability. Nowadays nets are supplied by the makers with the cork and sole ropes attached to the requirements of the purchaser.

WHITE SPOT An area 17 miles SE by E of Montrose where herring spawned during the month of August.

WULKS Winkles. These are still gathered along the seashore. Not to be confused with whelks, which can be seen in the decoration of the Buckie House in Anstruther.

YAWL Fishing boats under 35ft were generally classed as yawls and were powered by 15 or 30 H.P. Kelvin paraffin engines, or by sail.